I'm Off to College, *Now What?*

A Step-by-Step Guide to

Surviving the
First Year

Danielle Lieneman

I'M OFF TO COLLEGE, NOW WHAT? A STEP-BY-STEP GUIDE TO SURVIVING THE FIRST YEAR

1405 SW 6th Avenue • Ocala, Florida 34471 • Phone 800-814-1132 • Fax 352-622-1875
Website: www.atlantic-pub.com • Email: sales@atlantic-pub.com
SAN Number: 268-1250

Library of Congress Cataloging-in-Publication Data

Names: Lieneman, Danielle, 1995- author.
Title: I'm off to college, now what? : a step-by-step guide to surviving the first year / Danielle Lieneman.
Description: Ocala, Florida : Atlantic Publishing Group, Inc, 2017. | Includes bibliographical references and index.
Identifiers: LCCN 2017045538 (print) | LCCN 2017049878 (ebook) | ISBN 9781620231982 (ebook) | ISBN 9781620231975 (pbk. : alk. paper) | ISBN 9781620232477 (hardcover : alk. paper) | ISBN 1620231972 (alk. paper)
Subjects: LCSH: College student orientation—United States. | College freshmen—United States.
Classification: LCC LB2343.32 (ebook) | LCC LB2343.32 .L54 2017 (print) | DDC 378.1/98—dc23
LC record available at https://lccn.loc.gov/2017045538

Printed in the United States

PROJECT MANAGER: Danielle Lieneman
INTERIOR LAYOUT AND JACKET DESIGN: Nicole Sturk

Reduce. Reuse.
RECYCLE.

A decade ago, Atlantic Publishing signed the Green Press Initiative. These guidelines promote environmentally friendly practices, such as using recycled stock and vegetable-based inks, avoiding waste, choosing energy-efficient resources, and promoting a no-pulping policy. We now use 100-percent recycled stock on all our books. The results: in one year, switching to post-consumer recycled stock saved 24 mature trees, 5,000 gallons of water, the equivalent of the total energy used for one home in a year, and the equivalent of the greenhouse gases from one car driven for a year.

Over the years, we have adopted a number of dogs from rescues and shelters. First there was Bear and after he passed, Ginger and Scout. Now, we have Kira, another rescue. They have brought immense joy and love not just into our lives, but into the lives of all who met them.

We want you to know a portion of the profits of this book will be donated in Bear, Ginger and Scout's memory to local animal shelters, parks, conservation organizations, and other individuals and nonprofit organizations in need of assistance.

*— **Douglas & Sherri Brown**,*
President & Vice-President of Atlantic Publishing

Table of Contents

Introduction

You Got in, Now What?

It is the big day, the day that has been approaching for all of senior year. In the mailbox, there is a letter with admissions office in the top left hand corner of the envelope, right underneath the name of the university you applied to. Or, there is an email in your inbox with the news that will help you decide what the next chapter of your life will look like. You get nervous as you tear open the envelope or click the link. You close your eyes, unfold the paper, see the screen, and bam! Just like that your nervous jitters turn into cheers of excitement as you read "Congratulations, you have been accepted into this year's class of students!" Whether it is your first acceptance letter or final one, it is always thrilling to learn that you have added to the list of options for the next big decision of your life. After you re-read the letter, tell your parents, and do your happy dance, a whole new wave of questions hit you. You start to realize that the world beyond high school is coming up quickly and there are many uncertainties. Sure, college will be fun, but what will it be like moving into a new environment? How easy will it be to make friends? How will I choose a major? Are the movies and TV shows that depict college life accurately? This book will help to answer these questions and many more. Celebrate that letter and let's dive in!

Chapter 1

Planning and Preparation

After you have taken a second to congratulate yourself on this huge accomplishment, the next step is to plan for the future. Unlike students entering high school, new undergraduate students have a lot of preparation to do before they get to the university itself. There are dorm room or apartment items to buy, books to purchase, and family preparations to be made. These are exciting events, but try not to leave them until the last minute or else the fun could turn into stress. This chapter is here to help you figure out how to make the most of the time before you head off to college.

Before You Leave: The Summer Before

The summer before you leave for college is an interesting time. On the one hand, you've done it! You're a high school graduate! While you should definitely take the time to celebrate, this summer will also be full of responsibilities as you prepare to leave in a few short months. The biggest thing you'll have to worry about is a summer job.

College is expensive. Yes, you have tuition and room and board, but you will also need money for books, adventures off campus, and that poster you just have to have for your dorm room. This is where all that moola from a summer job can come in handy — you'll have money in your bank account, wallet, or piggy bank and won't have to ask mom and dad to approve every purchase. There are many jobs that are for the summer only, especially those through city governments and pools. Many city governments have jobs that require mowing public spaces, cleaning up debris, or working as an office intern. The local pool may be looking for certified lifeguards, but many need concession stand workers as well. Go to your local city building to see if they have any positions or search for jobs online, through websites like Snag-a-Job. Many parents look for nannies during the summer while school's out for the summer. www.care.com is a great resource for babysitting and nanny positions.

While it may seem counterintuitive, the summer before college is a great time to get caught up on your reading. In high school, if you did not read the books you were assigned you might have looked them up on Spark Notes or gotten away with not reading the material at all. This is hard if, not almost impossible, to do in college. The readings you will be assigned may be too obscure to find summaries of online or it will be expected that you go further in depth than any summary could provide. Depending on what kind of college you go to, there could be daily discussions over the material, and you will be expected to participate. Reading the majority of the books is also a good idea not only for learning, but also when it comes time to write papers. Having notes on the books will be extremely helpful when you are trying to find that quote to perfectly sum up the author's argument or support the thesis of your paper. For these reasons, consider reading a few books in the summer. Pick out two or three books that sound appealing and set goals on when you would like to read certain chapters by. They do not have to be works of Shakespeare or Montaigne, though picking out academic level material may help to accustom to the level of understanding expected. If you are into stories about dystopias then finding a Sci-Fi novel or rereading the Hunger Games will do. There's a novel you have been meaning to read for ages, but just have not gotten around to it? Perfect, divide up the chapters and get started! Pacing your reading now will help you to get into the habit of doing it for courses in college.

If you do not already have an account, consider getting a Pinterest. Yes, the crafting do-it-yourself site. Before you jump to the next paragraph, Pinterest has a lot of good ideas for college students. From inspiring dorm set ups to academic advice and everything in between, this site has a lot to offer. Life hacks from people who were in your shoes can make the life of an undergraduate much easier — take advantage of it.

The summer before college will most likely be equal parts fun and preparation — not just for the to-be college student, but also the parents of said student. They are getting ready for the child they spent over almost two decades raising to fly (or drive) out of the nest. If they seem stressed or upset, just know that it is because they know that they will miss you and are nervous for a life with a changed family dynamic.

The same is true for the rest of your family and friends. Make time to hang out with your friends, but also remember that your parents and siblings will miss you as well. Try to make time for both. Go to the park, see a movie, or any another activity that you both enjoy. Older siblings and parents who went to college may enjoy you asking questions about their experiences. Not only will your family appreciate it, but you will be glad to have these memories to look back upon.

Study Break! More students are leaving their home state to travel for university than ever. Public universities and colleges have almost double the number of out-of-state freshmen now than in 1986.[1]

Buying Books: How to Get Around the Costs

One of the most expensive parts of college (outside of room and board) is purchasing materials that you will need for class. These costs may include a computer, notebooks, pens, binders, highlighters, flash drives, and planners. One inevitable buy, however, is the textbook. Unlike high school, colleges usually do not provide the reading materials, so these will have to be bought. Every class is different, so the textbooks will vary as well. For example, your biology class may use two expensive textbooks while the English class you are enrolled in might require five or six paperbacks.

When beginning the hunt for textbooks, check the details of any merit scholarship or financial aid package you may have received. Some colleges and scholarships give out a book grant, which allows their students a purchase allowance at the bookstore. If there is no book grant or the bookstore does not have the material you need — a very real possibility, especially if you wait until classes have started — then it might be a good idea to look

1. Strayer, 2016.

at other places to buy from. Before purchasing the books full price from the campus book store, look around online. Many textbooks can be found used for a discount price online and most can be rented as well. More often than not, these prices are substantially cheaper than their new counterparts. Just make sure that if you rent that the books are sent back on time, or a late fee may be charged to the buyer. Textbooks can be bought or rented from sites like Amazon or Chegg.

When deciding whether to rent or buy, take into consideration what you want to major in. Most freshmen go to college undecided, and this is totally okay — I'll explain why in Chapter 4, so stay tuned. If you are pretty set in your choice of major though, this could play a role in whether you decide to rent or buy books. If you plan on majoring in Economics, for example, that microeconomics textbook might be needed in the future. But the materials for your chemistry class can probably be rented.

Also take into consideration the amount of highlighting or in-text notes you typically do. It is important to be an active reader in college, and writing in the material is helpful to look over for discussions and assignments. Keep in mind that book renting companies do not care if marking up their books helped you to achieve an A- on your paper. They will charge you a fee or even the whole amount of the book if they deem it unusable for their next customer. If you tend to mark up the text then consider switching to writing on post-it notes or using page flags instead.

Buyer Beware: What to Bring Versus What Not to Bring

There are many college pacing lists out there that tell prospective students what they absolutely must have for college to make their academic careers a success. These can be found at stores and all over the internet. The truth is, however, that some of these lists add excessive items that do not really need to be purchased at all. Items like bed lofts and an unnecessary amount of bed sheets are put on the list to increase purchases of these products. Many colleges do not even allow some of the suggested items in their dorm rooms. Before going out and shopping, make sure to check the list of banned items in order to not purchase items that will go unused. Showing up with a coffee pot, a microwave, and a pet iguana on the move in day may cause issues with the resident assistant if they are not allowed at the college.

A good general list includes:

- ☑ Bedspread
- ☑ Pillow cases
- ☑ 1-2 pillows
- ☑ 1-2 sets of sheets
- ☑ A lamp
- ☑ Toiletries
- ☑ Schools supplies (book bag, notebooks, pens, planners, etc.)
- ☑ A season's worth of clothing (depending on how often you plan to go home)

Of course, there may be different items needed or wanted based on the individual and the college. Additional items may include:

- ☑ Decorations (posters, pictures of friends and family, artwork)
- ☑ A coffee pot
- ☑ An arm pillow
- ☑ A mini fridge
- ☑ A TV

Also, it is good to note that bringing extra furniture, like a couch or futon, may seem like a good idea, but college dorm rooms tend to have a limited amount of space. If a roommate is involved, it may be a good idea to coordinate with them so you have a better idea of what to bring. This way you can eliminate bringing the same items if you plan on sharing.

See the appendix for a more thorough packing list.

The Day Of: Saying Goodbye to Family Members

Picture this, it's move in day and all the items have been brought in. After setting everything up and fussing over how your bed is made for the millionth time, it's finally the moment when you will have to say goodbye to your parents. They may get emotional and tell you how proud they are, or they might try to hold it in until the car ride home. Whatever the case, remember to be nice to them as this is a huge day for them as well. It may be you're the first to fly the nest, the last, or maybe even the first in your family to go to college at all. This represents a huge moment not only in your life, but in theirs as well. The kid they raised has become an adult!

Peer Perception: Jordan Richtmeyer
University of Florida, freshman

While college may seem like all fun and games, it can be stressful and a bit of a culture shock when you first arrive. When the day comes to move into your new home, saying goodbye can be hard and full of tears. I'm generally a family-based person, so leaving home sucked. I still even have some homesickness. I suggest making it more of a "see you later" than a "goodbye," since goodbyes tend to feel more final than a general term that just says, "I'll see you again." When it comes to being homesick however, the feeling after you leave can be a different story. Since I'm so close to home, I just go home. However, with a job and school, it's sometimes not that easy, so I FaceTime my family a lot or even just call them. I won't lie, there's been weekends when I've called my mom three times a day, every day, and it helped an awful lot.

So now you're prepared with the items and knowledge you need. You've said goodbye to your high school friends and your family. Now only four years of classes, finals, and fun stand between you and your degree.

Chapter 2

Settling In and Staying Focused

The First Day: To Syllabus and Beyond

Today's the day! You've bought everything you need, met your roommate, and set your stuff up in your dorm. Now all that's left is to actually start classes. You may be nervous to actually begin, but have no fear — soon enough you will have the hang of it. As for the first day itself, it may be a good idea to do some preparation beforehand. Unlike many high schools, most colleges have their classes held in different buildings, usually broken up by academic fields and departments. To make your first day easier, write down your class list and the building in which each one will be located in. Then you can walk to each class itself and know exactly where to go on the first day. If you have time, try and do this the day before classes start — if your campus is large, it might take a few hours to find where each class will be held. Make sure that enough time is allotted to get around to each class.

Try to give yourself as much time as possible on the first day. This depends on how long it takes you to get ready and how far the classes are from the dorm, but aim for about 15 extra minutes just in case something does not go as planned. It is also important to eat breakfast on the first day, even if it's just a granola bar or some fruit. Breakfast is especially important in college because some days will be extra busy, and it will help you to keep your energy up for class.

The first day of college classes may seem intimidating and nerves might present themselves. This is completely understandable, as it is a new environment and many first impressions will be made. However, if you are prepared it will help to ease any nervous feelings and set you up for a successful first semester.

An important thing to know about the first day at a university is the introduction of the syllabus. A syllabus is an outline of the course that will most likely have the dates of each assignment. It may also include the topic the professor will be teaching about in class that day. In college, the first week of classes is often known as syllabus week. During this time, professors will explain the syllabus for the course and the different assignments listed on it. Bringing a binder or folder to put your syllabi in for each class is a good idea, as you will be referring to it throughout the semester. This way you will not have to constantly have to look it up on online or reprint it.

The Importance of Studying

One of the biggest mistakes many first semester college students run into is not studying enough. The final grade is no longer made up of smaller assignments but instead only two or three grades over the course of a semester. It may be that the professor gives out other assignments, such as papers and projects. Nevertheless, even with this added coursework midterms and finals will decide the bulk of the grade.

Study Break! The best way found to study is to break up information into 20 to 30 minute chunks spread throughout the day, several days before you are tested on the information.[2]

If you are thinking, "No big deal, I'll just pull an all-nighter and cram the night before," then I have some bad news. An all night study session will not only leave you irritable for class the next day, but they also have been proven to lead to lower overall GPA's and forgetfulness. If the exam is the next day, staying up all night will cause you to be unfocused and absent-minded when you go to take the test itself. The best way to study is to do it repeatedly over a period of time. The term "I'll sleep on it" also applies to studying: Sleeping in between study sessions has been proven to help students to retain more information.

---

2. Texas A&M University, 2016.

College Myths Debunked
You Do Not Have to Go to Class to Make the Grade

In many college-esque movies, students do not go to class at all. They spend all day drinking, partying, and participating in other shenanigans. A disproportionate amount of their day is spent doing whatever suits their fancy. In Blue Mountain State, a TV show about football playing college students, they are constantly portrayed drinking and hazing each other. Not only are they not shown in class, but they are never shown playing football. In reality, as college athletes, they would have very little free or party weekends mandated by the team — especially during the season.

There may be students who spend many nights partying and less time in class. These are the same students that will be asked to leave come the new semester or school year. The truth is, you have to go to class if you want to make the grade. Some classes are easier than others, but no professor is going to throw A's around like confetti. If you slack off and skip class, it will come back to bite you. There may be days where you are tired or simply do not want to go to class. When this does happen, remember that your grades and goals depend on you putting in effort now. If this does not work, then picture class a different way: every class you skip is worth around $31-$390.

Of course, there are many variables, such as how often the class meets and what your tuition is, that make this number different for each student. But even at the lowest level, missing three classes already totals to $93. At the highest end it will cost $1,170 — not to mention the money being wasted on books that are never used. If gaining the knowledge that will be necessary in the future is not enough motivation to get to class, then the physical cost should be.

Courses are not created so that you can schedule them and never attend. They are not there for show. If the guys at Blue Mountain State were real college students, they would have flunked out a long time ago or been put on academic probation, losing their spot on the football team and any scholarships they had been granted. Make sure that learning is still your number one goal and that getting to class is one of your highest priorities.

This is not to say that an all night "get your life together" study session will not be had at least once in the next four years. There may be a time when you procrastinated or had too many other assignments to complete in a short time frame, but it's not something that you want to turn into a habit.

So what are some solutions? What other lifestyles could there be? Here are some tips for re-thinking the way that you study:

- **Do not procrastinate:** In high school, time may not have been seen as a coveted thing, but in college it is a precious resource. Have a research paper due in a week? You may think, "Oh no big deal, I'll start it in a few days." This is a problem because a week quickly turns into a few days and then a few hours. Do not put off assignments and, if possible, try to start them right away. This does not mean writing the whole paper the day the prompt is handed. Instead, start thinking about what you will write and make an outline.

- **All time is valuable:** A common trap that students fall into is thinking that shorter periods of time cannot be used productively. Let's say you have 30 minutes to an hour before your next class. This time in between classes could be spent mindlessly going through your social media feed or you could go to the library and start finding books for your paper. Even if you have less time than half an hour, it can still be used productively. You could look up possible topics for your paper online and draft your thesis. This time saved will be appreciated later when you can hang out with a friend or go to an event instead of starting your research.

- **Schedule time:** Set aside time in your day to concentrate on readings and other coursework. The amount of time will vary with the amount of work given on a particular day, so plan accordingly.

- **Putting priorities in place:** Saying "I'll go study in an hour" is easy. Deciding to actually stop binge watching that show on Netflix to start studying is another story entirely. After class you might have the urge to go straight to your dorm to decompress or hang out with friends. Try to avoid this impulse and get your work done instead. Studying after class is a great way combat procrastination and get a good portion of work done.

- **Take notes:** Notes are incredibly important. Not only do they help you retain the information from lectures, but they also are prime study material. Copying your notes is a great way to reinforce the material as well.

- **Purchase a planner:** Seeing your schedule visually not only helps you remember important due dates, but you may also realize there are certain times that are consistently free. Don't just buy a planner though — actually use it! Write down homework assignments, self-imposed deadlines, and any commitments you may have for an organization you're in. Even if you aren't the type of person who color codes and plans their day out to the minute, planners can still be helpful for keeping track of important days.

- **Make flashcards:** For exams and tests, it is vital to be an active studier. This does not mean glancing over the notes, but re-writing and re-reading information in order to retain it. One of the most effective methods of active studying is making flashcards. They also are a great way of self-examining what material you know and what you do not. If the instructor gives you a review guide, make it into a set of flashcards. If there is no guide, then make one out of any information in your notes or textbook that may be on the test.

- **Take breaks and switch subjects:** If you will be studying for a long period of time it's important to take short breaks. For example, if you have been studying for an hour and are in need of a break, then a 10 minute pause will be a good way to clear your head. Studying for 20 minutes and then taking an hour break, however, is not a good use of time. If you have multiple classes to study for, then try to switch subjects. Taking 20 minutes to work on an anatomy reading and then switching to work on another subject for a while will be helpful to keep focused.

- **Find a study spot:** When college students think of studying outside their dorm room, they immediately think of the library. Although the library may be the ideal study spot for some, it is not the only option. Even if your campus is small, there are many places that might work for you. Many colleges leave their academic buildings unlocked so student can use unoccupied classrooms. If you love nature, try studying outside. Sit in the commons or find a tree to sit under. Other options include on or nearby off campus coffee shops and restaurants.

- **Make a playlist:** Studies have shown that listening to music helps to keep listeners focused and engages different parts of the human brain. It is also useful in blocking out the humming of the person sitting a table away. Finding an album, playlist, or radio station that work for you is as simple as examining the music you already like. If you find that the lyrics are distracting but listening to classical music isn't your thing, give instrumentals of your favorite songs or movie scores a try. Apps like Spotify and Pandora are great for finding radio stations and specific songs. The app Eight Tracks is great for finding premade study playlists tailored to your taste in music.

Writing Down To-Do's and Goals

In the busy days of college, students can forget what they are working towards and why they are there, which is why an online scheduling device or that planner you purchased is definitely worth using — how else will you be expected to keep track of school, friends, and family? On days that are especially busy to-do lists can be quite helpful. Crossing off tasks may also serve as a stress reliever.

Study Break! Use your daily planner most effectively by organizing it by urgent tasks, habitual appointments, and time buffers. The most crucial element is to plan for enough time in the day to accomplish everything critical.[3]

Once in a while, step back and see the big picture. Write down a list of short-term and long-term goals. Short term goals might include applying

---

3. Wilson, 2017.

for a scholarships and internships or getting an A on your Spanish test. Long term goals are bigger picture aspirations that may include getting your dream job, owning a business, or living in the perfect apartment. During the more hectic and harder times of college, these goals can be useful to look at as a reminder of the dreams that you are working towards. It is a big possibility that these ambitions will change or evolve the longer you are in college — that is to be expected — but having a list of long term objectives will serve as a reminder for why you are pushing yourself now.

Managing Time and Stress

Between tests, papers, friends, and applications, college can make students gain stress like scout badges. With the limited amount of time and increased work load, it is easy to become overwhelmed. When this happens, remember your big picture. You could panic about the amount of work you have to do — or you could start working on it. That may sound simple enough, but it is common to put off work because it seems like too much or impossible to finish; the brain tricks itself into never starting. Depending on the time frame, there is a chance that everything will not get done, but having the majority of the work done is much better than none at all.

To avoid situations like this, use that planner you bought! This will help you see when assignments are due far ahead of time and plan accordingly. Using a planner is not only great for tracking what assignments and events are coming up; they may also help you to realize that multiple assignments are due on the same day and that work will be need to be done in advance to avoid a stressful situation.

If you are struggling in a course, it is far from the end. Many colleges offer academic help to their students. Whether it is inquiring about a tutor or a taking a trip to the writing center, there are many outlets for help. Don't let stress and time management overwhelm you to the point where it affects your ability to do well in courses.

Study Break!   Many colleges offer free tutoring or group study sessions to students struggling with a course. Check with your school counselor or college website to find out where and when these services may be held.

Learn to turn down requests, social or otherwise. There are going to many opportunities to hang out with friends or volunteer for a service day, but only one to get a good grade on an assignment. Being social and involved is important — so much so that we have a whole chapter dedicated to it later — but know your personal limits. If you need time alone to decompress or study, take it and do not feel bad. This will not only make you a better student, but also a better friend. During the first semester in particular, it can be hard to turn down invitations, but remember that making the grade and learning come first. Classes, learning, studying, and health should be higher on the list. Parties, club meetings, and watching Netflix should be given a lower priority.

Another type of management is that of stress. Stress is easy to accumulate in college, so managing it is of upmost importance. There are many possible outlets for decreasing stress and everyone will have a different approach. Finding the most effective activity to decrease stress might involve some trial and error, but whatever outlet you choose should be relaxing. A few distressing options include:

- **Coloring:** You may be thinking, "Coloring? I haven't picked up a crayon since I was a toddler," but many find this an effective way to forget about their anxieties. Coloring and sketch books are portable and can be taken anywhere. With the recent adult coloring book craze, there are almost an unlimited number of options. From mandala patterns to Harry Potter and Game of Thrones, the choices are limitless. Want a more ironic or satiric option? There are many adult coloring books making fun of adult coloring books or mocking recent political events.

- **Sketching/Drawing:** This option is like coloring, but gives freer reign to the creator. Doodling in class may not be the most effective use of time, but taking a break during studying to draw some fantasy character or a favorite landscape may help to relieve some stress (and improve your skills as an artist).

- **Exercising:** It is important to work out for many reasons, particularly because it is a great way to clear your mind. Exercising to be healthier will leave you less stressed and more focused. A quick disclaimer though, exercising with the goal to lose a certain amount of weight can cause more aggregation and be counterintuitive to both goals. Eating healthy and working out are important, but you should focus on feeling good, not looking differently.

- **Journaling:** This is the grown up version of that diary you kept in middle school. You may write about your crushes if you wish, but journaling is an excellent way to organize your thoughts and talk about the day's events. Writing about your life is also a nice way to document your experiences in college. The activities you did today may seem simple, but future you will enjoy remembering your college years via your journal entries.

- **Meditating:** If you have never tried meditating before, this destressing activity (or lack of activity) could be for you. Most people think that meditating is not for them, but once they try to it, they never turn back. New pastimes do not always come easily to everyone, and meditation is no exception. Sitting quietly may seem simple enough, but when you get to it thoughts can invade your brain at a rapid pace. It takes time and practice to get to the point where you can meditate without examining the images that appear. Meditation becomes an incredibly useful tool when you reach this point. Thus, finding relaxing music and trying to meditate could be well worth the effort.

- **Reading for fun:** What? Reading even more? Are you crazy? That is a possibility, but some students actually find reading novels outside of class to be a way of reducing anxiety. There is probably at least one book you have been meaning to read, so finding a nice space to drink some tea and read may not be too terrible of an idea after all. If reading yet another book sounds too terrible to even attempt, then consider getting a magazine subscription or seeing if the campus library has magazines to check out. Reading out about the latest scientific discovery or celebrity break up may help your brain unwind.

There are thousands of activities out there that you could try. If playing an instrument helps to calm you down then consider bringing it with you to college. Creating memory boards or scrapbooks could be a fun distracter as well. The list of distressing possibilities are as numerous as the coloring book options. Finding the anxiety reducing pastimes that best suit you are key to a successful freshman year and can be a lot of fun to figure out.

Peer Perception: Brianna Murphy
Grove City College

Self-care helps keep you at your best during a very important time of your life. Grove City College has a counseling center that is free to students and can be instrumental in self-care for certain situations. When I'm stressed, I find an empty dance studio and dance, or sometimes I'll go on a run. I have found that eating meals with friends can help lower stress because doing so forces you to slow down and breathe for a little bit. For managing time, at the beginning of each semester, I write down all tests, exams, papers, homework, etc. in a planner and plan ahead for each item. This preparation helps to keep me from cramming for tests or pulling all-nighters on papers. And don't be that person who pulls all-nighters. It will not be worth it. Sleep is important.

I start studying right as the professor talks during the lecture. This is why attending class is important. I pay attention, ask questions if I have any, and I write notes with paper and pencil. Paper and pencil notes are generally better than computer notes. Most people can type really fast and keep up with the professor, but most people cannot write as fast as the professor speaks, so writing forces you to actively sift through the oncoming material and write down what is important. This process will help you recall the information better when you study for the exam or a final. It is not uncommon for me to see freshmen take their notes on computers, but then switch to paper and pencil after the first exam. If you have the time, feel free to type up your notes after class. Then you have a clean organized copy and will have an even better recall for the test.

Homesickness: How to Deal With It

Even the most college-ready academics are going to get homesick at some point. No matter if you appreciated or had severe disdain for high school, there will be a point where home is missed. Whether it is for your family, childhood friends, or your old room, there will be a longing for something familiar and comfortable. This nostalgia is normal and to be expected from students leaving home for the first time. It is nice to remember the past, but it is not healthy to ruminate on this homesickness. If you are in your dorm room when it hits, try to get out and go on a walk or study in another space. Another remedy could be finding a friend to hang out with. Distractions and a change of scenery are typically helpful remedies to this homesick feeling.

Study Break!   If you're feeling out of place your first year
of college, you are not alone. A UCLA Higher Education study
found 69 percent of incoming freshmen felt lonely their first year.[4]

Talking to your loved ones will also help stave off the homesickness. Set up standing time to call or Facetime the family members or friends you are missing each week — and write it in your planner so you won't forget about it!

Some cases of homesickness last for minutes, while others could be whole days. During these longer periods, attempt to see the big picture of why you are at college and remember that the time you have here is fleeting. The best investment for your future is to be working towards a degree in order to have a better opportunities and quality of life. Find a few quotes that really inspire you and try to remember them during these times. It is easier said than done but homesickness can be beat. It just takes some effort and a reframing of the situation.

Peer Perception: *Alyssa Prado*
University of Florida sophomore

The first time leaving home was hard; tears were definitely involved on both ends. Going home and then back to school gets easier every time. It helps that I try and send a text to my parents every day and try to call at least once a week. I think it's important to realize that the college experience isn't just about getting away from our parents. If we think being independent is hard, it is a million times worse for our parents. The best advice I can offer is to talk to them, and put in the effort. The same goes for friends. The ones you want to keep in touch with will stick around no matter how little you talk to them. A text every here in there will make the distance seem that much shorter.

---

4. Wong, 2015.

To battle homesickness, I try to talk to my parents at least every day. I don't have the time to call them every day, and they understand that, so I make it a point to send a text just talking about something I did that day. When I do call, I make sure it's at a time that I can dedicate a substantial amount of time to my family. I think it helped that I didn't make it a point to go home a lot right when I started. I try to limit my trips home, so I don't get attached all over again.

It's extremely important to not burn yourself out. It can happen faster than you think, and oftentimes without warning. It's important to not only keep your physical health in check, but your mental check as well. When I get stressed I take a break from whatever it is I'm doing and do something I know I enjoy. For me, I love to read. I try to stick to reading bits of a book I know and love, so I don't have the urge to drop everything and finish a new book. I try to time my breaks and after my time is up, I'm usually good to start working again. If not, I'll start the process over!

In high school, I would study the day before an exam and be fine. College has been a whole other ball game. There have been exams where I only study the bare minimum the day before, and I get by with a decent grade. But I know had I truly committed, I could have done better. When I take the time to study for an exam, I'll start a few days before. On the first day, I break the days up by chapter and try to master those subjects. The following days I start by quickly reviewing the previous chapters before moving on. The day of the exam, I'll have a final review of all the subjects. I get bad test-anxiety, so I find it better to spend the time right before the exam doing things that relax me.

The first couple weeks of college will be the hardest, but also the most exciting. Everything will be new and terrifying, but don't worry. Before you know it, the new will become the ordinary. You'll have a routine and know where your classes are. You'll have a favorite study spot and will have figured out how to effectively study for that brutal calculus class. Now that you're all settled in, let's see what we can do about getting you some friends!

Chapter 3

Making Friends and Having Fun

Depending on how long you went to the school district you graduated from, there is a good chance that you may have known the other students in your class for many years. Maybe you were with them from middle school or even kindergarten. For better or worse, you are now no longer with the same group of people. By its very nature, college is a place where you are exposed to different people from varying backgrounds. You may not realize it, but each person is full of opportunities for not just friendship, but learning and personal growth as well. It is more than likely that there will be students from different states and countries with experiences and cultures completely different from your own. Even if most students are from the same state as you are, there will still be many chances to learn about experiences unlike your own. Not to say that you should treat each person you meet like a textbook, but be aware that they may do somethings differently than you. These differences may be foreign to you and that is okay! College is all about broadening your horizons — and that includes ways of thinking about things that seem concrete.

Opportunities to Meet New People

College will be chalk full of occasions to meet new people. During orientation and move in days you will see so many new faces, so if you get the chance, try to start a conversation. Putting yourself out there can be a scary thing to do, even for the most extraverted of people. Remember that every person you meet is going through the same thing: They have to make new friends in a new environment just like you are. Your friend group will likely change multiple times — especially over the course of the first semester — but it will be nice to have a few people that you can talk to and hang out with, even if you gravitate towards different people as your college career progresses.

Study Break! If you want to start making new friends during move in day, consider leaving your dorm room door open after unpacking. This is a universal signal to say your room is open, and to come and talk to you.

The RA's (resident assistants) in your dorms may occasionally plan activities for your hall. Getting involved in these events is a great way to meet other freshman. These students will be your neighbors for the next year, so getting to know them might not be a bad idea. If anything, it will make asking to borrow a fork to eat your ramen with less awkward.

The friends you make in college could become some of your closest and most meaningful relationships that you build throughout your life. The time you spend bonding with these friends may possibly be some of your fondest memories, so enjoy meeting as many people as possible. It is easy to become settled in with one friend group as you progress into the semester, but try to make an occasional new friend or two. There are so many opportunities to become closer with people and you do not want to miss these because you think you have enough friends already.

College Myths Debunked
First Week Friends Are Forever Friends

There are many movies that portray that the people a freshman meets in their first few weeks will be their best friends for life, like in Pitch Perfect. In the first few minutes of the movie, Anna Kendrick's character is off on her college adventure and, as many freshman do, she attends the involvement fair her university has thrown. As much as I encourage attending involvement fairs, I do not recommend walking into them with the idea that you will find the perfect fit on the first try. College students often sign up for many clubs at involvement fairs and then end up participating in a few that they truly enjoy and want to dedicate time towards. The same can be said about freshman friends made in the first few weeks of college. There will be many new faces that you will meet at orientations and freshman events. For Anna Kendrick's character, this meant that she found her niche and her friends within a matter of days. Many freshman, however, take a bit more time to find the fellow students they really click with. There will be many people who come and go within the first month or two of college, and this is completely normal. During this period of time students are trying to figure out who they connect with the most, and it may take some time to figure this out. Although there is a chance it may happen, do not go into the first day thinking that you have to find a group of best friends right then and there to hang out with for the entirety of college. You will find those people who you will be forever friends with, just not necessarily in the first week.

I also challenge to-be freshman to go out of their comfort zone, even when they do find friends they cherish. Continuously meeting people and making connections is a big part of the college experience, and no one wants to look back at their four years regretting that they stayed in a box. You have friends you have not even met yet, so even when you do have friends you love, I implore you to continue searching for those connections.

The Importance of Getting Involved in College

College is all about learning and growth, and the best way to do this (other than going to class) is by getting involved. This means attending involvement fairs and finding a few organization or clubs that you may want to get involved with. These can be activities that you were involved in high school, or completely new pursuits. Do something that you always thought about, but never had the opportunity to. Have you wanted to write for a newspaper, but never got the chance? Then attend a meeting and write an article. Did you think about learning to fence, but did not have the time or resources in high school? Pick up a lance and try it out (just be sure to put a mask on first!) There will most likely be booths for organizations that you have never heard of. If they sound interesting then check them out. Simply talking to the people at the booth or signing up for the email list does not equal a lifelong commitment.

Trying a few new things will help you to learn about new ideas and connections that you may have not been exposed to otherwise. Even if you do not stick with a particular club, it is worth trying to find out if it is for you. Best case scenario, you find a new passion. Worst case, you attend one meeting and move on to try to find another activity.

Finding your niche, or the place where you best fit, in the slew of activities on a college campus can be intimidating. It may be that the first club meeting you attend will be the perfect place for you. More realistically though, it could be that it takes you until the second semester or even second year of college before you find the activity you like best. But to find your niche, you first have to go out and look.

Study Break! The University of Florida alone has over 1000 clubs for students to explore, this is mirrored in the majority of colleges, so don't sweat trying to find the perfect club for you right awcy.[5]

Attending Events

One of the best ways to find out where your interests lie is to attend campus events. Whether you have found an organization to be a part of or not, these events can spark your interest. Apart from events put on by clubs, colleges will often have speakers come to campus to discuss various topics. For example, during my first semester of college my campus had a former NFL player, a high fashion model, a women's rights activist, and many more come speak to us about their lives and different issues that they have faced in their careers.

---

5. Student Activities and Involvement, 2017.

Service and community organizations typically host some sort of event throughout the course of the semester. If your college has a Habitat for Humanity chapter, they might have weekend builds and will bus you to the site of construction. Even if you have never had an interest in building so much as a Lego house, creating a life changing structure for a family can be quite rewarding. Other service organizations to become involved with include Big Brothers Big Sisters, Love Your Melon, Salvation Army, Food Recovery Organization, and America Reads. Each college has different organizations, so check out some that you might want to get involved in.

Study Break!   Some clubs and organizations have a point system to stay a member in the club, attending events and completing service activities often fulfills this requirement.

It also may be beneficial to attend a meeting or event of a culture that you have interest in learning more about or is different from the one you identify with. For example, the Global China Connection chapter at my school held an Autumn Festival and the International Student Association threw a festival for the Hindu religious holiday of Diwali. These events were great sources of learning and helped me to better understand the cultures that my fellow students and friends come from.

Another type of event that you can attend is those pertaining to your major or a major that you might be interested in. Some departments, especially those in the humanities, have various meet and greets where you can talk to professors in that field or seniors in that major. Throughout the course of the year, seniors will be presenting the research they have conducted during their time at the university. Attending these events may help you to decide if a certain major is something that you might like to pursue.

Being involved in campus events will not only broaden your horizons, but also help you to have a more enriched college experience. Going out and meeting people with similar interests can spark new ideas and help you to make discoveries that you may not have otherwise.

To Join or Not to Join: Greek Life

Joining a sorority or fraternity is a point of confusion for many college students. Some students may already have an affiliation with Greek life because of siblings or parents. Maybe you are planning on joining the second you get on campus or maybe you are totally against the idea altogether. Either way, it is good to note some pros and cons on both sides.

College Myths Debunked

If movies and TV shows had it their way, every party ever thrown on a college campus would be put on by a Greek chapter. This is the whole premise of Neighbors, Neighbors 2: Sorority Rising, and House Bunny. Though Greek organizations do sponsor parties, they are far from the only organizations or people on campus to do so.

There is also this underlying tone in movies that every single person who has walked the college portion of Earth is either a fraternity or sorority member or a stereotypical nerd. The TV series Greek is the epitome of this: The main character tries to go from "geek to greek" — a clever play on words with no basis in fact. Another example of nerds versus jocks can be found in the movie Revenge of the Nerds. These movies and TV shows show Greek Life as necessary to fit in at university, but nothing could be further from the truth.

Each college is unique and the number of students who choose to join Greek life will be unique as well. This is evident when you look at the percentage of students involved at different colleges. Ohio Northern University only has 24 percent of its male students affiliated with a fraternity, while Centre College has closer to 40 percent. The majority of colleges fall below the 24 percent mark when it comes to male student population participation in Greek life, so the idea that you have to join Greek life to fit in is a media-fed myth with no basis in reality.

There are many misconceptions about Greek life. Watch any movie about college life and you are bound to find at least one reference to either pledging, illegal substance use, or wild parties. Joining a fraternity or sorority does not mean that you can slack off or change your major to party expert. Greek life is about joining a sisterhood or brotherhood that is bigger than oneself, and oftentimes there are required study hours and community service. After pledging to a specific organization, you have an instant family and possible support system. That being said, there are negative aspects about Greek Life that should be considered as well.

One of the biggest reasons people are unsure about joining Greek Life is the financial cost. Dues are paid to the organization and are typically hundreds or thousands of dollars a semester. While this may seem high, many times these dues include meals and help subsidize events for the whole chapter. There will also be times where you are expected to buy gifts for members — usually for your little "brother" or "sister" — and other items like t-shirts throughout the course of the year, but many times these are optional. There is also a large time commitment that you are expected to give, but many Greek students are involved on campus — if they can juggle multiple organizations, who's to say you can't?

Study Break! In 2012, there were nine million students involved in their college sororities or fraternities.[6]

Each Greek organization has a different reputation, so ask around to see which one fits your personality the best. Although many college's have policies against hazing, some Greek organizations still have hazing rituals that they force new members to participate in. Do some research to see which fraternities or sororities seem to be the best fit, but don't only listen to rumors and reputations around campus. Just as with any organization or large group of people, Greek chapters can be judged by one person or one rumor.

If you are still on the fence by the time your college has rush events, it's still worthwhile to attend. These events are noncommittal and give you a chance to meet members and learn about the organization. If you still aren't sure, don't feel pressured to join. In many Greek organizations it is hard, if not impossible, to switch fraternities or sororities after you have been initiated. That means if you later feel like you hurried into the decision and identify with another fraternity or sorority, you will not be able to join. Waiting

---

6. Glass, 2012.

until next rush season will give you more time to figure out which affiliation is the best fit or if you want to join at all. No matter what you decide, make sure you are basing your decisions on facts and not on stereotypical depictions of Greek life.

Peer Perception: Katherine Jones
University of Florida sophomore

Making friends can be difficult, especially if you do not know anyone at the university to start with. The main lesson I learned my first semester is to feel the fear of judgment or rejection and go for it anyway. I cannot count how many times I have been absolutely terrified applying to be a part of an organization or signing up for a club. Feel that fear, expect some discomfort, and trudge through. Little actions make the largest difference. In my experience, complimenting someone is a super easy way to push yourself out of your comfort zone and start a conversation. You never know where the conversation could lead to.

I am involved in a sorority and write for an online publication. Finding clubs is all about finding people you would like to get to know and work with. Getting involved in organizations on campus takes a little bravery and persistence. The first club you join may not be the right fit and that's okay. Keep trying to seek out your passions and you'll meet new people that share the same goals and interests. They will be a source for more opportunities. I love writing, so when I saw openings for an editorial position through one of my sorority sisters I applied and now I am meeting new people and doing what interests me.

Roommate Tips: How to Pick and Get Along With Your Roommate

Picking a roommate can be hard. Many colleges today have systems in place to help you find the best possible match. These are typically automated systems that pair you with the person who answered questions the same way, and are most likely what will be used if you choose to have a random roommate.

Study Break!   More students are finding their college roommates through Facebook groups or digital apps, such as RoomSync or StarRez, than waiting for random selection by their university.[7]

Another option is to go on social media to meet students in the same entering class. The university you are attending may have a Facebook page set up specifically for this purpose. Go on and see people who are looking for roommates as well and try to find the person who seems most compatible. No matter which route you choose, some good questions to ask potential roommates include:

- Do you stay up late or wake up early?

- How organized/clean are you?

- Are you open minded about other points of view?

- How often will you be in the room?

- Do you snore or are you a light sleeper?

- How do you feel about having people in the room?

- How do you like to resolve conflict?

- What are some of your pet peeves?

A more thorough roommate questionnaire can be found in the Appendix.

The worst mistake you can make when trying to find a roommate is to have someone else do it for you or lie about what you are truly like. Fill out any questionnaires honestly and be truthful with yourself. Do not put that you

---

7. Chuck, 2015.

are completely organized if you are in fact quite messy. Being paired with a neat freak will only make things harder on both you and your roommate if you are fine with being disorganized.

Do not feel shy about asking potential roommates necessary questions. Try to talk to your new roommate via text messaging, calling, emailing, or through social media direct messages. Ask them what they like/dislike and how they might want to have the room set up. This person will live in the same room as you for a whole year and while you do not have to be best friends, it is important that you have respect for one another.

A quick disclaimer about rooming with your best friend from high school: do not do it. You may be close now, but more often than not this ends when two people room together. Just because you know everything about each other does not mean your habits will line up. It may also make it harder to bring up potentially awkward subjects and cause drama. Even if things work out perfectly, there is a good chance that having a best friend as a roommate will hinder you from going out and meeting new people. Having your friend from high school to fall back on may end up hurting you in the long run.

Studying and Socializing: Finding Balance

Attending events and making friends are important to college life, but do not forget the way you stay in college: your grades. It does not matter if you are the most involved and well liked student on campus: if you fail out, you will not be allowed to come back. Your main goal should always be to learn the most and get the best grades possible.

Do not set unrealistic expectations for yourself. Going into college expecting to get a 4.0 GPA, do all the readings, and still attend every event on campus is an unachievable goal for even the highest overachiever. Set a

GPA goal for yourself, but make sure to make it challenging and reachable. If you are taking a class that you feel will be hard for you, then do not make the goal to get a 100 percent in that course.

The same is true when finding balance between friends and socializing. It can be hard to turn down friend invites to hang out and study instead. But remember that your future of making friends at college relies on you actually being there. Over-socializing instead of studying can make your grades plummet. Setting yourself up for success in the first semester can really help to boost your GPA throughout your college career. It does not have to be one way or the other, however. Invite friends to come study with you — just make sure that you are actually being productive for at least most of the session.

Conversely, make sure that you are not always studying or in your dorm room secluding yourself from the outside world. Everyone needs their down time, but make sure that you are also going out to connect with others.

Finding balance between friends and studying can be difficult, but it is a necessary part of college life. Learning to manage time and prioritize are two important attributes that collegiate need to gain to find the best combination to accomplish their goals.

Peer Perception: Delaney Herper
College: University of Florida junior

Getting involved is very crucial in making sure that your time at college is enjoyable. I am really only a part of two clubs, one being the Pre-PA (physicians assistant) Association, and I joined the club to get more information on getting into PA school. The other is the Hooked to the Book club — which my friend Kylie started — and it's a good stress reliever because it's all about reading and relaxing from school. I also have a regular job which is another way of getting out and doing things. Having a job, balancing school, and extracurricular activities takes a little getting used to. You just have to figure out when you'll be able to do your homework and studying every time you get your work schedule. The nice thing about living in a college town is that most places are pretty lenient on work schedules because they understand that most of their employees are also students.

Another piece of advice: take care of yourself. With the hectic life of a college student it is very crucial to make sure that you're okay. It's important to take care of yourself because if you don't, things tend to get away from you, like your grades. When I get stressed I tend to sit down and read a couple chapters of a book. I've also really gotten into adult coloring books lately, so I'll spend some time on those. I'm probably the worst person to ask about time management because I'm a major procrastinator and am always studying at the last possible minute. I'm usually a crammer, so I tend to do all of my studying in one night. Recently found some friends who make studying a little better, and I will study with them a few days before the test.

There's no doubt about it: making friends is hard and stressful, but it's also a lot of fun. The people you meet in college have the potential to be lifelong friends — even if they aren't, you'll still have a whole lot of fun. It's important that you make an effort to make friends early on. If you're nervous, just remember that everyone else is looking to make friends too!

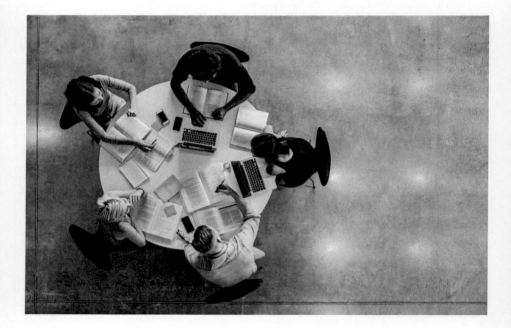

Chapter 4

Choosing a Major

When you start telling people that you've decided to attend college, be prepared for the onslaught of questions: What's your major? What are you studying? What classes are you taking? What are you interested in? The list goes on and on, and there are no easy answers to these questions — especially when it feels like your answer is signing on the dotted line to give your soul away. Whether your life's dream has been to serve as an ambassador to the UN and you know that your major will be political science with a minor in Arabic and sustainable development, or you don't even know what you want for dinner tonight, let alone what you want to do for the rest of your life — take a deep sigh of relief when I tell you this news: the major you declare upon entering college really isn't all that important.

College is full of opportunities to learn about yourself and your interests; the classes you take, the clubs you join, and the people you meet will all influence you. It's expected that you will change your major. In fact, many colleges are reporting that even a majority of students change their major: University of Laverne reports 50-70 percent[8], Ohio State University esti-

---

8. Laverne, n.d.

mates 50-75 percent[9], and the University of Florida narrowed it down to 61 percent[10], just to name a few. In the event that you don't have any clue what you would want to do, don't worry, your admission won't suddenly be rescinded. Many colleges have got your back and offer an "undeclared" option for incoming students.

Undeclared Doesn't Mean Unprepared

Most of you know that you can begin your college path with an undeclared major. This simply means you have not yet decided what area you will major in. Depending on the classes that you took in high school, most of your first year, if not your first two years, will consist of general education classes: English Literature and Composition, Calculus, American History, and Biology. The benefit of signing up for general education classes when you have an undeclared major is that you will not be wasting any time or money by taking classes that will not fulfill graduation requirements.

College Myths Debunked
You Have to Have Your Life Planned Out Now

Rory from Gilmore Girls always knew what she wanted to do with her life. Go to Harvard (or Yale), major in journalism, travel the world, and write hard hitting stories. Before she was 15 she had her life completely figured out. The seven seasons of the show follow her completing each step of her journey to this goal with relatively few obstacles. This is great for her, but what does it mean for people who do not have their life planned the second they are born? Are they doomed?

The answer is no. Not knowing what you want to do at age 18 or 19 is completely reasonable. Some people know by this age that they want to be a neurosurgeon, a teacher, or a lawyer. Most, however, have no idea what they want to do. Or better yet, they have too many

---

9. Ohio State University, n.d.
10. Simon, 2012

ideas and would like to be a teaching neurosurgeon lawyer so they do not have to choose.

College has so many options that it is easy to become overwhelmed. The main thing to remember is that you should enjoy whatever classes you take. I know what you're thinking: "Enjoy classes? She must be crazy!" Of course there may be a few general education (GE's) credits that you may not love, but overall you should be interested in the courses you are taking. While this may not mean that you love every minute you're studying or are in class, it's important that you genuinely are interested in the subject. If you do this, you will eventually find something you love. There is a good chance that even if you know exactly what you want to major in that you may change your mind. Some people go in as dance majors and come out with a degree in chemistry or vice versa. Or maybe you end up having a double major in both. You never know what you are going to end up wanting to do and this is okay. As long as you keep your mind open to all the possibilities, you will figure out what you want to do.

However, many colleges are starting to recognize the benefits of coming into college without a specific major declared and have begun to rename the undeclared classification as "exploratory." For example, at the University of Florida, there are three different tracks available: engineering and science, humanities and letters, and social and behavioral.

Selecting classes with an undeclared major

Use your first year and maybe even your second year of school to decide on your major. Experiment with different classes. Pick subjects that interest you and do not be afraid to try new areas and explore your options — many classes will fulfill the general education requirements that you need to take anyway. If you've always found astronomy fascinating, even if you think you would never major in it, try it out. Although you may not decide to be an astronomy major, you might choose it as a minor or just pick up some quality star gazing tips — which will come in handy for future dates, I might add. Plus, it's better than physics, at least in my mind — sorry to all you future physicists out there, but I never could bring myself to care about the rates of falling objects!

Study Break! An Education Advisory Board study in 2016 found 83 percent of students who finalized their major in their second semester or later graduated, while students who finalized or never switched their major from their first semester had a graduation rate of 79 percent.[11]

Pick classes that match your personality and interests. If you like debating current events and politics, try Introduction to International Relations or Introduction to Political Theory. If you are always trying to figure out why people act the way they do, look into Psychology or Sociology. If you've

11. Straumsheim, 2016.

always been a fan of theatre, take Theatre Appreciation. Allow yourself the freedom to explore your interests. If there is ever a time to try new things, this is the time and place to do it.

Not having a definitive answer to that ever-present question about your major can be discouraging, especially when you're experiencing pressure from friends, family, and even your teachers to declare a major right away. They pressure you because they want the best for you. They want you to have direction and focus; to quickly be on the path to graduation. Be sensitive about their concerns, but tell them not to worry. You are not wasting time or their money by not declaring a major. Explain to them that you will be mostly taking general education classes in your first semester and even first year of school. Tell them that you are trying to explore your options fully and that when you do decide on a major, you want to make sure it is the right decision. Not knowing and even switching your majors in the first couple years of college is perfectly normal and not at all harmful to your college graduation goal.

If not knowing your major the first year is a problem for you — which I don't think it should be — you should know that there is help out there for you. Colleges have a career center that will help you explore options for different majors, and, more often than not, will try to help you take your interests and strong subjects and translate them into a major. Check out jobs that interest you and look to see what degree they ask for in the job posting. Search through **www.careerbuilder.com** to find possible careers. Ask your professors and advisers what kind of jobs you could expect to get if you major in certain areas. Most of all, take your time deciding and make sure you are making the best decision. If you find a job that interests you, ask experts in that field what they majored in and then ask them why. Ask them if they could do it over, if they would still choose the same major.

Make a list of majors you are considering. Write down why you think you would want to major in each of those areas. List the pros and cons of each one. Consider the following questions:

- Do you like the job options the major tends to offer?

- What is the salary range of entry-level people in the field you are considering?

- Would a graduate degree be required to make yourself marketable or earn a decent salary?

- Would you find the required classes interesting?

- Would you want to join a club with only people in that major as members?

Coming into college undeclared is almost a blessing in disguise. It allows you to explore different classes and opportunities that might not have been on your radar otherwise.

For those of you lucky enough to know your major coming into college, it's important that you keep an open mind and explore opportunities too.

If You Already Know: Planning Ahead

Maybe you are one of those students who have known since they were five years old exactly what they wanted to be when they grew up. Maybe you are certain you want to major in Psychology or Civil Engineering; that is good to hear. My advice to load up your first year or two of general education classes still holds true. Schedule one or two classes in your major during your first year. Realistically evaluate the classes. Do you truly like the field as much as you thought you would? Are the classes coming easily to you or are they the hardest classes you have? Are you interested in the courses required for your major? Do not let the emotions of wanting a declared major get in the way of realistically evaluating whether the major is right for you.

Do not be afraid to change your mind. Your first and second year of college should be the time when you explore yourself and your interests. Even if you have been set on being a dentist your whole life, you may find your interests have changed. Be open and honest with yourself about these possible changes. If you have a change of heart, do not feel locked into the major you have declared. It is common practice to switch your major during college. (Author confession: I changed my major from political science and public relations to advertising with a minor in English, with quite a few unofficial changes in between!)

Alongside your major classes, use the same advice we gave to undeclared majors: take classes in subject areas that have always interested you. Always been curious about art history but you're dead set on being an economics major? Take Art History 101. The worst that will happen is you'll find yourself annoying anyone you ever go to a museum with as you teach them the correct process for analyzing the piece of art.

The good news is that if you've tapped into a previous unknown love of art history, but your parents insist that you get a "practical" major, you can always declare a double major or minor.

Choosing a Double Major or Minor

At some point in your college career, you may decide to pick up a minor or a double major. Some students choose a minor later on in their college experience because they happen to have almost enough classes in an area to qualify. Other students plan a minor from day one because they are particularly interested in a specific subject area. If you are planning on having a minor, make sure you are doing it for the right reasons. A minor will not help all that much in your career path. Sure, you will list your minor on your résumé when you first graduate from college, but beyond that first job, you will likely never list it again. And to be honest, employers are not that wowed by minors. If you do decide to pick one, make sure it is an area that you enjoy, and get a minor for that reason alone.

Peer Perception: Alyssa Prado
University of Florida sophomore

I think I'm one of the lucky ones who went into college knowing exactly what I wanted to do and that hasn't changed (yet). I also knew that with a degree in Business Management, I would be able to follow my dreams and keep my options open. I decided to pick up a minor in English because of my love for books. I truly missed taking English classes and learning about literature! With this minor, even more doors are open to me should I choose to take a different direction in my career.

As for you, overambitious double-major types, good luck. Double majors do not quite equal double the work, but make sure you know what you are getting into. Discuss your decision with your adviser. Chances are you will not be able to graduate in four years with a double major unless you came into college with a lot of Advanced Placement or Dual Enrollment credits. Look at the advantages and disadvantages of having a double major. Ask yourself why you want or feel like you need a double major. How much will it help you in your career path? Are you just equally interested in two areas? Should you try to decide on one area and maybe make the other area a minor instead? Carefully look over the requirements for both majors and ask for tips from your advisers, professors, and field experts.

Study Break! Only 12.5 percent of people aged 20 to 29 had a double major in 2015, although research in 2011 also suggests that a double major can earn a 3.2 percent premium benefit over those with only one major.[12]

Now let's say that after all those art history classes, you decide that the only career that will bring you fulfillment is being an art historian. Those pesky economics classes are just a distraction. You'll be pleased to know that changing your major is an option.

A Major Change

As a freshman in college, you will be assigned an adviser. If you are undeclared, you will most likely be assigned a general adviser. This adviser may be a professor, a member of the advisement staff, or a counselor. If you have declared a major, you should be assigned someone familiar with your major as an adviser. Depending on the size and organization of your school, your adviser may be a professor in your major area or an advisement staff member that specializes in your major.

Your adviser is your first contact to help you register for classes. She will help you select courses, assist in the registration process, let you know how to add or drop classes, and even assist you in exploring and possibly changing majors. Your adviser should be concerned with more than just registering you for your first semester of classes though — he or she should want you to succeed throughout your college career and help you find a major that you love.

---

12. Makridis, 2017.

Study Break! The Education Advisory Board found that students went through an average of 2.5 majors before they graduated.[13]

Be prepared before your meeting. Study (yes, I said study — there's homework even outside of class work now) your college's course catalog. For any major(s) you are considering, highlight courses that you've already taken and still need to take. Look over your college's graduation requirements and make sure your adviser is fully aware of the requirements as well. Ask questions — lots of them! This is an important decision and your adviser's job is to help you.

That being said, do not rely on her to know everything. As a college freshman, you will have to take responsibility for your own education, and that means making sure you get to graduation on time. Consult unofficial advisers. Talk to older students. Ask them about what classes they took their freshman year of college. Ask their advice on which classes are best taken early on and which ones should be saved for later years. If you have an older sibling or friend in college, even if it is not your college, ask their advice too.

13. Straumsheim, 2016.

Peer Perception: Kat Jones
University of Florida freshman

You never know where the conversation could lead to.

My first semester I was a declared General Business major and later switched my major to Public Relations. This transition was one of the hardest and most confusing times of my educational career so far. The actual act of changing your major is seamless and requires only one step. You simply meet with an adviser of the school that houses the new major you want to declare. One tip I can offer when changing your major is to meet with an adviser more than once. Prepare a list of questions about the major you wish to charge into, including what critical tracking courses you have missed and need to make up or if any credits you already have can be used towards this new major.

I decided to switch because when I looked ahead at my four-year plan, I was not excited about the classes I had been scheduled to take. What helped me pick my major was the feeling I got when I looked at the classes required for that major. If I wasn't looking forward to those classes that told me it perhaps is not the right fit.

The bottom line is that you will have to make your own decisions when it comes to your college education, major, and class schedule. To make the best decision, consult many sources and form your own opinion.

Deciding to change your major is a big decision. Make sure to explore all of your different options. Explore job opportunities in any major(s) that you decide on. Make sure that, whatever your decision, you pick a major that will lead to a career that you will love doing every day.

Fully Loaded: Scheduling Classes

Now that you know or do not know your major and have met or at least talked with your adviser, you are almost ready to schedule your first classes. Notice I said "almost." You should spend much more time preparing to register for classes than actually registering. Most schools offer online registration, so the actual time it takes to sign up is just a few clicks of a mouse. The hard part is not registering but knowing what classes to register for. Your adviser can help you with this process, but there is still a ton of work you need to do to make sure you are getting the best class schedule possible.

Once you are ready to start creating mock schedules, which you will review with your adviser before you register, take note of the following key items:

- **Know your lifestyle:** Are you a morning person or a night owl? If you cannot wake up before noon unless dragged out of bed by wild horses, do not schedule that 7 a.m. chemistry class. Pick class times that best match your lifestyle. In some cases, you may get stuck with early morning, but if you have a choice, look for classes you know you will not be sleeping through every day.

- **Register early:** In other words, register as soon as you can. Freshman level classes can fill up quickly. Do not be stuck taking classes you did not want, at times you did not want, with professors you did not want, just because you procrastinated scheduling your classes.

- **Know your graduation requirements:** Have I drilled this point in yet? If not, here it is again. If you do not know your graduation requirements, how can you expect to graduate? I know, that is four years away still, but do not forget that is the goal. Keep your goal in mind when scheduling your first classes.

- **Plan ahead:** Look beyond your first semester. Try scheduling for the entire year and even your sophomore year. Of course, your schedule may change, but looking ahead will help you to not miss out on classes that may only be offered at certain times of the year or have prerequisites that are only offered in the fall semester.

- **Do not overload — or underload — your schedule:** It is your first semester of college. Classes are harder than they were in high school, and you have more responsibilities to balance. Do not try to take too many classes and overwhelm yourself. You will need to adjust to college learning and an increase in homework and studying. Taking too many classes too soon will add more stress, and you'll have enough of that already. This does not mean that you should take the bare minimum of classes either. Most colleges have requirements for minimum class hours to be a full-time student. Meet that requirement the first semester but do not try to impress anyone (including yourself) by taking more than what is required.

- **Diversify your schedule:** Mix up your classes so you are not overloaded with hard classes, too many reading assignments, or labs. Read the course descriptions to find out more about the class and, if available, check out the syllabus ahead of time. If you can download course syllabi before you register, check out the due dates of major assignments and look at when finals are scheduled. Try not to schedule classes with the same exam dates; it will be overwhelming. Diversify your schedule by how hard you think the classes will be. If you are a math whiz and you know it, schedule a math class. Add to it an English class, even though you cannot write your way out of a paper bag. Schedule some comfortable classes along with ones you know will challenge you.

- **Balance:** Some students think class meeting time is most important. For some, the professor makes the difference. Others say you should be most concerned with your level of interest in the class. So, what factor is most important in scheduling classes? The answer is all three. You should weigh all three factors and decide which one is most important to you. The answers will vary for every student. The ideal class would be one at a good time, like 2 p.m., with a professor who is both challenging and entertaining, and covers a subject that you just cannot wait to learn more about. But how often is that going to happen? Chances are you will have boring professors, far too early class times, and be stuck learning a subject you could not care less about. At least consider these factors so that you get classes closer to the ideal while you are registering for your classes.

- **Foreign language:** Is a foreign language a graduation requirement for your college or major? What do you mean you don't know? Have you not been studying the graduation requirements? Well, you should know if it is required. If so, and if you took a foreign language in high school, consider taking the same language the first semester in college. Do not wait until you have forgotten all your "Como estas" skills.

- **Take a chance:** Do not stick with just the classes you are comfortable with or that you know you will need to graduate. Of course, you want as many classes as possible to count toward your graduation requirements, but you are not stuck to only scheduling those classes. If you are trying out different majors, pick a class in a major you think you might like or just pick one that sounds interesting. If it is something too off the wall, you may want to ask around a bit before you jump in, just to make sure you know what you are signing up for.

- **Ask older students:** If you know upperclassmen who have taken some of the classes you are interested in taking, ask them about the class. If you know they have taken a class with a professor who is teaching a class you are thinking of scheduling, ask them about the professor. They can offer their opinions — you may agree or disagree. You may love a professor they hated. A class someone tells you is boring may have been changed or may be taught by someone new and could be completely different than it used to be.

- **Allow time in between classes:** In high school, you took all your classes in a row, then went home and studied (maybe), and then woke up the next morning to do it all again. College is different. Classes are usually offered only two to three days a week. The classes are longer and require more work during and after class. Back-to-back classes can leave your head spinning in no time. Schedule your classes with good breaks in between. This break will allow you to clear your head, get in a little extra studying, or even knock out some homework while it is all still fresh in your mind.

- **Do not overload your days:** It might be tempting to schedule all your classes from Monday through Thursday and have a three-day weekend every week, but that may not a good idea. Your week before Friday will be so intense that you may not be able to do anything on Friday except sleep. You will not have time to study in between classes during the week either. Opt for a schedule with Monday or Friday as a light day, but do not try to pack all your classes in a four-day week.

- **Take freshman orientation:** I am not referring to your first-day orientation after you have moved in, and your parents are still hanging around. Many colleges offer a class for freshmen. This class may be worth little or no credit or it may even be required. Either way, it can provide a wealth of knowledge for freshmen. These classes help you transition into college, get to know your own college, offer study tips, and let you meet a bunch of other freshmen all in one blow. They are usually pretty easy and have assignments like writing your mission statement for college.

- **Avoid the easy A:** Do not pick classes just because you think they sound easy and you think will give you a GPA boost. Take classes to learn — that is the point of college. Easy classes are a waste of time (unless they happen to be part of your graduation requirements) and money. You should strive to take classes that will help you learn something and will result in a well-rounded education.

Picking your major and scheduling classes are stressful tasks, but they are some of the most important tasks you'll have before starting college. Getting an education IS why you decided to go to college, isn't it? Make sure that the education you end up getting is one you'll love to make a career out of one day. Explore the course catalog, take interesting classes, and maybe find out something about yourself you didn't know before.

Chapter 5

Healthy Habits

The Freshman 15: that terrifying part of college where you eat pizza and bagels for every meal and gain 15 pounds your first year. Whether the Freshman 15 is a myth or statistically proven is still under debate, but the reality is that you will be at risk to pack on the pounds in your first year of school. You will most likely be getting the majority of your meals from the dining hall — a place that is not known for its fine dining — and unless you are still living at home, you will be making your own decisions about what you eat, how much you eat, and how often you eat — most likely for the first time. It's hard to say no to every free pizza or ice cream that's offered at the various club meetings you'll be attending. Surprise! The cost of getting involved is your waist line. Relax, *I'm only kidding*. Being healthy is a balance. I promise, you'll be able to eat that free pizza and not gain the dreaded Freshman 15.

Freedom Also Means Responsibility: Taking Care of Yourself

Cafeteria dining in college might turn out to be much different than you are used to from high school. You most likely will have more selection and with any luck, it will be quite tasty. Most college dining halls are unlimited buffet-style dining. There is no one scooping out your portions — even if there is, there's no one telling you to not get a second or third portion. There's also no one forcing you to eat that salad, but it's probably a good idea. You will have to monitor your own serving sizes and what types of food you eat. Just because your school serves pizza every day, it does not mean you should eat it that frequently. Leave the pizza for the club meetings and use the dining hall to eat healthy, or at least as healthy as you can get.

Study Break! 63.9 percent of students in 2016 reported to only eating one to two servings of fruit and vegetables per day when the average recommended diet calls for four to five servings.[14]

Remember the food pyramid from your ninth grade health class? You'll actually get to put that knowledge to good use. You should be thinking about the basic food groups every time you enter the dining hall or go shopping for dorm room snacks. Include vegetables with your proteins and grains. Try to eat fruit for dessert instead of getting ice cream or chocolate cake.

You can pretend that carrot cake is a vegetable, but that your body will be treating it like the (delicious) cake it is.

Stay away from fried foods, or at least significantly limit the amount you eat. Try to avoid eating anything with added sugars — and that unfortunately includes the double mocha you've been thinking about all day. While you should limit these foods, it's important to allow yourself a few splurges or else you'll eventually give into your cravings — moderation is key to a healthy lifestyle.

---

14. ACHANCHA, 2016.

Use college as a time to try new foods and explore diversity in your eating habits. If your campus offers different ethnic style foods, give them a try. You may be surprised at what you end up liking. College is the time to expand your horizons.

Plan ahead for healthy meals and snacks. Dietitians recommend eating smaller meals more often instead of having three huge meals a day. Avoid the temptation of the vending machine down the hall, and pack your dorm room mini-fridge and cabinet with healthy snack foods like:

- Yogurt

- Popcorn — without the butter!

- Pretzels

- Granola bars

- Trail mix

- Rice cakes

- Peanut butter

- Baby carrots

- Celery sticks

- Fruit (fresh and dried)

These are all easy to eat while studying or on the run in between classes. Try to keep your dining hall meals healthy and allow for the snack food splurges when you have a craving for something sweet or otherwise unhealthy. Buy mini candy bars or single-serving snack foods for those times when you just can't say no to the thought of mac and cheese — but do not eat them on a regular basis! Your schedule is likely to be irregular while you are at school and so your meals might end up being irregularly scheduled as well. Do your best to eat small healthy meals and snacks every few hours. Eating more often keeps your metabolism up.

Peer Perception: Kat Jones
University of Florida Sophomore

Watching what you eat is probably one of the hardest aspects of going to college. Late study nights are a major culprit for greasy pizza and fast food munchies, and dining hall food is sub-par when it comes to offering appetizing healthy choices. The first steps I would say to do are get a basket for organization and a mini fridge. What I tried to do my first year was stock up on healthy snacks that I ENJOYED eating. I always kept berries, Greek yogurt, carrots, and oatmeal in mine for a good breakfast. Protein bars, protein shakes, and bananas are good options that don't need to be refrigerated! Whenever I would go late to the library or want a snack between classes, they were easy to eat on the go and satisfy any cravings I had. Another tip would be to get a water bottle. Try setting a goal to drink at least four refills per day to keep hydrated. If you do happen to have a meal plan and eat in the dining hall, stick to the salad bar and bring your own container to fill with nuts and dried fruits for late night snacks.

Speaking of metabolism, many college students become dependent on caffeine to keep them going throughout the day. With energy drinks, soda, and coffee available at every corner, it is easy for any student to become addicted to super-caffeinated beverages. I know it's tempting, but beware of overloading your diet with caffeine. Drinking water will actually help you maintain a healthy weight and may even help you lose weight. Make it a goal to drink the recommended 64 fluid ounces of water every day. Buy a water bottle that holds exactly 64 ounces of water and fill it up every day. Take it around to class with you so that you always have water handy. Use the caffeinated beverages for only those times you truly need it — they dehydrate you and can affect your sleeping schedule, both of which can affect your weight and energy levels. Drinking water before meals will help you feel fuller earlier and help prevent overeating.

Healthy Eating on a Budget

It always seems like healthy food is more expensive than its junk food counterpart, doesn't it? When you start to tire of cafeteria food, which is bound to happen sooner or later, you may start buying food at restaurants. Buying food at restaurants when you are on a tight budget usually means you are eating fast food. You know that fast food is not healthy; you do not need me to tell you that. But it is cheap, and as a college student sometimes cheap outweighs healthy. Maybe you do not have to make that decision though. There are ways to eat healthy not break the bank at the same time, but that requires going to the grocery store.

When shopping at the grocery store for those healthy snack foods to keep in your dorm room, look for the store brand items instead of name brands. You will save money, and you won't be able to notice a difference in taste. Price compare on sizes of boxes. Even though you will not eat a whole box of graham crackers in one setting, you might be getting more bang for your buck if you buy the larger size than buying two smaller size containers.

Study Break!   The key to eating healthy on a budget is to plan, plan, plan. Create a meal and snack plan, compile a grocery list (and stick to it) and always check the local grocery ads for the weekly sales in order to best tailor your shopping to your money saving goals.

Coupon clipping is not just a hobby for old ladies. You may be able to buy those name brands you truly enjoy by scanning through the coupons in the paper. You can also request coupons for your more expensive favorite foods for your care packages from home. Always be on the lookout for deals, and don't be afraid to stock up as much as possible.

It may seem like healthy meals come at a cost, and while they will be more expensive than the 98-cent box of Kraft mac and cheese, they don't have to break the bank. Craving avocado toast, like the millennial you are? Instead of splurging at brunch, smash up some avocados and toast some bread yourself. (Psst, as a fellow millennial, I can confirm that it tastes amazing with some Sriracha and tomato slices thrown on top.)

Other cheap and filling meal options include:

- Tuna salad — great on sandwiches or as a dip for crackers and pretzels

- PB & J — not just for your kid sister

- Rice and beans — surprisingly filling

- Scrambled eggs — add some frozen vegetables for even more nutrition and flavor

When you do inevitably eat out, find the best deals. Local restaurants know that their main clientele will be college students with very little money, and they frequently have specials to draw in business. If the pizza place down the road has a special every Monday night, be sure to schedule your pizza nights for Monday — although that doesn't mean you should eat pizza every Monday, as tempting as that is. If you need to have food delivered to your dorm room for late night study sessions, shop around for those places with the cheapest (or better yet free) delivery charge. And eat those leftovers. Buy a meal larger than what you can eat in one sitting and save half for lunch the next day.

If you decide to host a get together or party at your dorm room, do not plan on buying the food for all your friends. Ask your friends to bring a side dish so you are not footing the bills for all the food. You might also be surprised at how much food you are stuck with at the end. That means more leftovers, so you could be making out on some free food in the long run.

Fad Dieting, or How to Lose Weight Quickly and Gain It All Back

Eating healthy is not about dieting. It is not about South Beach or Atkins or any other popular fad diets. Stay away from diets that promise huge weight loss in extremely short amounts of time. Dropping a lot of weight in a short period of time is not healthy and often leads to regaining it just as quickly as you lost it. Be sensible and keep a diet that you can stick to long term. If you have nutritionists on campus, ask them for advice on eating properly.

Carbohydrates (carbs) are not your enemy. Calories aren't your enemy. Fat isn't your enemy. Sugar isn't your enemy. Are you sensing a pattern here? No singular food group or nutritional fact is the enemy. Balance your diet between the major food groups. Look at the total fat content, the calories, the carbs, the fiber. It's important to read the nutrition labels on as many foods as you can.

The secret to healthy weight loss isn't hard: If you consume fewer calories than you burn in a day, you will drop pounds. If you take in more calories than you can burn in a day, you will gain weight. You know you consume calories with food and drinks, and you burn calories from exercise. Yup, it's time to finally put those Nikes to good use.

Exercise Schmexercise

Whether you are an exercise buff or a couch potato, it's important to make an effort to maintain a regular workout schedule. Your college will most likely have a gym on campus that you can use free of charge — this actually means that you've already paid for it with your student activity fees, so why not put it to good use?

Make it your goal to visit the gym three to five times a week and vary your workout so you do not get bored and stop going. A lot of campus gyms have fitness classes that are also free. Some popular favorites on my campus were hip-hop fitness, Zumba, yoga, and total body — a class that usually left me feeling like I couldn't walk on those infrequent times I went to the gym.

Learn from my mistakes, and don't overdue your workouts. Infrequent intense workouts may do more harm than good. They'll leaving you sore and feeling like there's no point to working out. Keeping a regular schedule of moderate exercise is the best way to get fit and stay healthy. This type of exercise will help you look your best, maintain a healthy weight, and help reduce your overall stress.

Study Break! In 2007, the American College of Sports Medicine and the American Heart Association recommended 30 minutes of moderate exercise on five or more days of the week, and 20 or more minutes of intense exercise three or more days of the week.[15]

Focus more on cardio when you are crunched for time, which will almost certainly be more often than not. Weightlifting is good but if your goal is to lose weight or reduce your total body fat, cardio is the way to go. Muscle weighs more than fat; so, if you are building muscle and the number on the scale is rising, do not worry. Concentrate on reducing body fat instead of lowering the number on scale. Aim for an ideal pant size instead of setting a goal weight. If your school's fitness center offers classes or counseling, take advantage of the programs. If they have a body fat measurer available, get tested and use your body fat percentage as a goal.

Ask for help from the fitness center staff. If you are not familiar with the gym equipment or you walk into the gym and feel lost, ask if someone can help you develop a personal workout schedule. Once you get started, you will find it easier to maintain a routine. Find a few different pieces of equipment that you feel comfortable on and vary your workout between them. Load your phone with favorite workout tunes and jam out while you burn calories — and earn those steps for all you Fitbit wearers out there.

Look for a workout partner. While you may not want any of your new friends to see you looking sweaty and red-faced, it'll help keep you motivated if someone is there to hold you accountable. Look for someone with

15. ACHANCHA, 2016.

a similar schedule to you, then team up to go to the gym. You can encourage each other when one of you does not feel like going. Having a workout buddy also makes the gym more fun! You can gossip in between reps and complain about the professor who keeps laying on homework during game day weekends. Find ways to motivate yourself and your workout partner so that you are encouraged to keep up with your schedule. Avoid using food as a reward though — telling yourself you can eat ice cream every day that you workout will defeat the purpose of working out and set you on a path of bad habits, not good ones.

If working out is not your thing and if you just cannot seem to fit in at a gym, find other ways to get exercise routinely. If your campus is bike friendly, start biking to class. Take your bike to the store or your friend's house instead of driving or taking public transportation. Time yourself when biking to your favorite locations and try to beat your best time. If biking is not feasible, try power walking to class. Find a form of exercise that is both effective and fun. If you like sports but are not college sport caliber, find a recreational or club team. You do not have to be like David Beckham to play soccer on a rec league. If you like the outdoors, find a hiking group you can join. If you were a world-class swimmer in high school, find out open swim times at your university's pool.

Working out and eating healthy should be something you enjoy, not a burden.

Avoiding Illness and Getting Medical Attention

College dorms mean close living quarters and are an ideal setting for diseases to spread like wild fire. Colds, flu, and more serious illnesses can spread easily from room to room. Knowing what illnesses to watch out for and how to protect yourself from contracting these diseases will help you keep yourself from being a victim of a college dormitory illness.

Vaccines and Preventative Measures

Before you enter college, you'll be required to have certain vaccinations — and for good reason. If your college does not require the meningococcal vaccination, be sure to get it anyway. This illness can be serious and has a quick onset. Meningococcal meningitis causes death in up to 20 percent of teenage cases — that includes you 18-year-old college freshman — and severe health problems like kidney failure.[16]

Its symptoms can easily be confused with the flu:

- Fever above 101.4°F [38.6°C]

- A rash pinkish in color

- Nausea and vomiting

- Muscle aches

- Sudden, severe headache

- Confusion

- Light sensitivity

A stiff neck, a headache, and sensitivity to light are key symptoms differentiating meningitis and the flu.[17]

The close living conditions of dorms make college campuses an ideal host for epidemics of this disease. The good news is there is an effective vaccine available to prevent this illness. For around $75, the vaccine protects against the bacterial meningitis infection. A viral form of this disease can also be contracted and is not protected against with the vaccine. However, the viral form is less severe and often requires little or no treatment for the patient.

The flu vaccination is another vaccine that all students should consider, but it's one that many people blow off. Ask your doctor or campus clinic whether or not you are a good candidate for this vaccine. Although the

---

16. American Academy of Pediatrics, 2016
17. American Academy of Pediatrics, 2016

vaccine cannot protect against all strands of the flu, it will offer added protection against this nasty bug, which runs rampant on college campuses.

Study Break! Florida State University experienced over a dozen cases of hand, foot, and mouth disease in Fall semester 2016, which launched a campus wide hand washing campaign.[18]

Of course, you will be exposed to other diseases that do not have vaccines available. The common cold is likely to circulate your dorm at least two or three times a year. To avoid catching the latest dorm room bug, take care of yourself all year long. Wash your hands with soap and water often — there is no better way to prevent the spread of illness. Always wash your hands before you eat and after you visit any common area. Make sure to thoroughly wash any kitchen utensils you use. Other ways to stay healthy include not smoking, maintaining a healthy diet and exercise program, and reducing your stress — as much as you can for a college student anyway.

Medical Supplies

No matter how many precautions you take against getting sick, you will most likely end up catching something while you are in college. With any bit of luck, it will be nothing more than a common cold or stomach virus that passes quickly. When faced with an illness for the first time away from home, you almost certainly will find yourself wishing someone were around to take care of you and feed you some of Mom's homemade chicken noodle soup. Even without your mom, help is out there. Your college campus will have healthcare clinics and trained staff to help you get through these times. Plus, calling home to whine to Mom is still allowed, of course.

---

18. Schweers, 2016.

Having a few supplies stocked in your mini medicine cabinet will help you deal with minor illnesses. Buy a first aid kit with the necessities: band aids, cough drops, decongestants, and headache and fever reducers. If you are commonly afflicted with certain illness (for example, colds or sore throats), be prepared for those illnesses striking in college. Keep the medications you have learned work best for you. Buy a thermometer so you can take your own temperature when you are feeling feverish. Knowing if you have a fever will help you decide if and when you need professional medical attention. If you call the school clinic and talk to a nurse about your symptoms, it is always helpful if you can tell them what your temperature is.

Having a can or two of chicken noodle soup stocked away for times your tummy is upset or you feel the flu coming on is always a good idea, even if it's not as good as your mom's. If you have other similar comfort foods that you can easily keep on hand, stock those items as well. If you are sick, you will not feel like running to the store for a bottle of Sprite or Gatorade or to get a bag of pretzels.

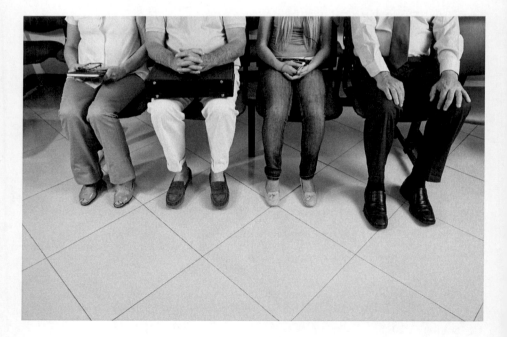

When Enough is Enough — Visiting the Clinic

If you get sick and your mini medicine cabinet is not just not doing the trick, seek medical attention before it gets worse. Know what your medical insurance policy is and be familiar with whom to call in case you are sick — before you are faced with an illness. If you have campus insurance, you will be seen by the campus medical staff. If you are on your parents' insurance policy, find out who you can see local to your campus when you get sick. Most on campus clinics accept a majority of insurances, so be sure to check ahead of time.

If you do not already, be sure to get annual physicals to ward off more serious or long-term conditions, like high blood pressure or cholesterol.

Do not rely on pre-med students or nursing majors to diagnose your illness. Bear in mind that they are in school just as you are. While they may know more about illnesses than you do, they are not trained professionals. Seek real help when you are sick. Even more importantly, do not rely on WebMD or other online resources to self-diagnose your illness either. You might have a cold, or you could end up convincing yourself you've got a brain tumor!

If you get medical attention, listen to the treatment you are given. Don't skip pills or stop taking your medication as soon as you start feeling better, or else you'll find yourself fighting off strep throat all semester.

Study Break! In 2016, 21.6 percent of college students reported having to be professionally treated for allergies with the past 12 months. This was also the most prevalent common illness treated.[19]

---

19. ACHANCHA, 2016.

If you are attending college in an area of the country different from where you are accustomed, you may end up suffering from allergies that you never had before. There are more allergy medications available over the counter than ever before, but you will still need to consult medical professions to determine which medication is best for you. Some medications may cause side effects like drowsiness, so it might take a few tries of medicines to find the best one. Your doctor might give you samples at first to determine which medication you should take. Instead of spending too much money trying different over-the-counter meds, ask a doctor to recommend something for your specific symptoms and allergies.

It's inevitable that you'll get sick in college: with that many people sharing a living space, how could you avoid it? You may also gain some weight and not eat as healthy as you could have. Both are okay. Getting sick is a normal part of life — and so is eating all that free pizza and mac and cheese on late night study sessions. Just be prepared and find a balance.

Chapter 6

Safety First

We've all seen those Hollywood depictions of crazy college kids who never go to class and use college as an excuse to party. While that may be true for some people, I'd contend that they're the minority. If college were really like movies depicted it, no one would ever graduate!

That being said, you will find yourself confronted with alcohol, drugs, and parties. If you're anything like I was in high school, this will be an entirely new experience for you. Some of you on the other hand, might already be rolling your eyes and thinking about skipping ahead to the next chapter. Don't get ahead of yourself though — do yourself a favor and at least skim it. You might even learn something!

College Myths Debunked
Making Friends Means Drinking

This is one of the biggest misconceptions of college. Of course there are parties and people drink, but it is definitely not the only way make friends. Typically, you make friends and then (if you choose) go to a party. Alcohol is often seen as a way of bonding and parties as a "typical college experience." There is this mentality in movies about college about "learn hard, party hard", but you never actually see the learning part (and no, the "bend and snap" in Legally Blonde does not count as learning).

The truth is, these portrayals are often a great exaggeration of what really happens in college. People do go out on the weekends (and sometimes Thursdays as well), but not everyone does. Some people may stay in or go out and not drink at all. Unless you go to a dry campus (and even then), you will probably run into alcohol consumption at some point. If you choose to participate in any of these events, make sure you do so with intelligence and do not participate because of peer pressure. Do not go with the intention of having the stereotypical summer blockbuster version of what Hollywood thinks college should be. Your college experiences should be just that — uniquely yours. And whether that experience includes the party scene is completely up to you. You will have friends either way.

Study Break! An average of 49 percent of students surveyed in 2016 admitted to drinking alcohol at some point within one to nine days before taking the survey.[20]

It's not just you that can be affected either. Your family is sending you to school — often they're even paying for it. Do them a favor and be responsible. After all, they're going to be affected, too, if something serious happens to you.

As a college freshman, you will be confronted with more choices and more opportunities than you ever had in high school, and you will not have mom and dad around to tell you "no" every step of the way at the threat of a month long grounding. You will have to make your own decisions about what parties you should and should not go to, how much, if any, you should drink at the party, and whether you will take part in any other mind-altering substances. Making decisions about how you will handle these choices before you find yourself in a situation will help you prepare

---

20. ACHANCHA, 2016.

for how you want to respond to the offers and make responsible decisions without the peer pressure affecting your choice. Remember, you are here to learn — even if Hollywood makes college seem like it's all fun and games.

Party Like It's 1999 — or Like It's College

First things first. Should you even go to that party your roommate's boyfriend's friend invited you to? Well, that depends. Is it a weekend or a school night? Have you finished all your homework? Do you have an early morning class? The answer to this dilemma will vary every time an invitation comes up. It's important for you to enjoy college and have fun with your friends — just as it's important for you to get good grades and pay attention in class.

So let's say you do go to that party. You're confronted with loud music, even louder people, and a whole lot of alcohol. Suddenly everything you learned in D.A.R.E. comes flooding back to you. You just know that your parents will somehow find out — or even worse, the cops will.

Chances are that as a freshman in college, you will not be 21 years old yet. So legally you are not allowed to drink. Now, I am not naïve enough to believe that all of you will wait until your 21st birthday to take your first sip of alcohol. Actually, many of you may have indulged in a few underage drinking parties before you even left for college — told you I was not that naïve. So, let's talk about underage drinking honestly.

Drinking underage may not seem like a big deal, but it can have big consequences. If you get caught with alcohol, you can get charged with what's called a minor-in-possession, an MIP, which is a misdemeanor charge that will appear on your record. Many employers and graduate schools check public records for these types of charges, so this could have very real consequences. If that wasn't enough, you could get in trouble with the university if was on the college campus. For example, at University of California, Berkeley, "alcohol citations from the UCPD, the Berkeley Police Department, or the California Department of Alcoholic Beverage Control **may** be subject to additional sanctions for violating the Code of Student Conduct, depending upon where the citation was issued.[21]

Let's say you decide to partake — it is college after all. So here's my recommendation: follow beer commercial advice.

I know what you're probably wondering what this crazy lady talking about, but just bear with me. You have seen beer commercials on TV, or I am assuming most of you have. The end of the commercial asks viewers to, "Please drink responsibly." Plan ahead: think about how much you'll drink, if at all, and arrange for transportation home. If you attend a party within walking distance of your dorm, have a group of friends ready to stumble

21. Anonymous, 2017

home with you when you leave — it's important to not walk alone at night. Recall those other commercials about how "friends do not let friends drive drunk." Listen to that advice as well. Do not drive, or let someone else drive, even if you both swear that you've "only had like two and that was like an hour ago" and "you're perfectly fine." It only takes one time for something to go horribly wrong.

Drinking responsibly in college, despite your age, also means knowing when to stay home and when to go out; know yourself. If you do not have the self-discipline to only have a drink or two at a party and stop, and you have a final the next day or a paper you need to write, sit this party out. There will be plenty of parties; you do not have to go to every one that you get invited to. Be adult enough to select which parties you should go to and stay home on the nights you know you have too much studying to do already.

Study Break! The National Institute on Alcohol Abuse and Alcoholism defines binge drinking as bringing the blood alcohol content level above 0.08 grams. This typically happens after drinking four or more drinks of standard alcohol content or higher for women and five or more drinks of standard alcohol content or higher for men, and both with the span of two hours or less.[22]

Know your tolerance. If you have never drunk before — and no, a glass of wine at Thanksgiving doesn't count — you will not know your tolerance. Heck, even if you did drink in high school, you probably still don't know your tolerance yet. Take it slow and do not overdo it. Do not try to keep up with upperclassmen just to try to prove something. More than likely, the only point you will prove is why you should not drink more than you can handle — and you will almost certainly come to that realization when you

---

22. NIAAA, n.d.

find yourself hugging a toilet, too sick to move. Spending the night puking is not cool, no matter how you slice it. To help a low tolerance, make sure to never drink on an empty stomach and drink glasses of water in-between glasses of alcohol. If you think you'll look lame drinking water, put your water in the same type of cup most people are drinking out of and when people ask you what you are drinking, tell them straight vodka. Some people will blindly believe you and others will see through your fib, but with any bit of luck, you'll at least get a laugh from your response. To tell you the truth, most people don't care whether another person is drinking or not.

The common rule of thumb is not to drink more than one drink every hour. This rate was created based on studies showing that the average person can process one ounce of alcohol every hour. I know it's hard to believe, but one shot of tequila has just as much alcohol as the 12-ounce Solo cup of beer or a glass of wine. Keep track of how much you're drinking to better pace yourself. Drinking more than one drink every hour will lead to more of a buzz, for sure, and maybe a few other unexpected twists in the evening.

So what happens if you have a lot more than one drink every hour? Well that depends. This next section will walk you through it.

Alcohol Poisoning and Medical Help

Lemme guess. That punch probably tasted like Kool-Aid, and you and your friends kept commenting on how you "can't even taste the alcohol so there's probably like nothing in it." You kept drinking glass after glass, maybe even took a few shots. Eventually, your body will stop being able to process alcohol and you, your roommate, or your friend — whoever took all those shots — will potentially start vomiting and could even pass out and become unresponsive.

So what exactly happens to your body when you're consuming alcohol that leads to this point? Let's discuss.

Alcohol is actually a depressant — counterintuitive, I know — and technically a poison. While you're partying it up on the outside, alcohol is actually depressing nerves and receptors in your body that control essential functions like your gag reflex and breathing — not to mention your decision making abilities.[23]

After enough drinks, your body is finally will start to expel the poison from you, and that's when the nausea kicks in. If you've reached this point, you have alcohol poisoning.

No one wants to be the person to admit that maybe things went a little too far, but think about it. What's more important? Being uncool at a party or potentially saving someone's life?

If you notice that anyone's state is continuing to worsen, immediately assess the situation. Look for critical signs and don't just think they'll sleep it off and have a killer hangover in the morning.

Critical signs of alcohol poisoning include:

- Confusion and stupor

- Unconscious and unresponsive

- Vomiting

- Seizures

---

23. College Drinking Prevention, n.d.

- Slow or irregular breathing (fewer than eight breaths per minute and 10 seconds or more per breath respectively)

- Hypothermia[24]

If you notice any of the above signs, it's imperative that you call for medical attention.

When you're in a high stress-situation like described above, it can be hard to think straight. If you're around other people, they'll be sharing their opinions about what to do and no one will want to make a decision.

Someone will probably mention that calling for medical attention could get the the person in trouble and all of you in trouble — you are all under-age, after all. While it may seem inappropriate and selfish for someone to mention the prospect of getting in trouble, it is a valid concern. Many

24. College Drinking Prevention, n.d.

campuses have a Medical Amnesty program to alleviate those worries. What this means is that if someone's life is in danger from alcohol and/or drug use, the students involved will not face any repercussions as long as they alert the proper authorities. Look on your university's website to see if your school has a similar program. Your R.A. will be familiar with the policies specific to your school.

Sexual Assault

It's an unfortunate reality that this section must be included in a book about your first year of college. College should be a time when you're finding your identity — a real, grown-up version of yourself — but unfortunately, college-aged individuals, particularly women, are three times more likely to be victims of sexual assault.[25]

I know we all have ideas in our heads about campus sexual assault: it's someone slipping a roofie in your drink at a party or it's someone grabbing you as you walk home from the library at night. It's never someone you know, and you never even had the chance to fight back or say no — but those aren't the only cases.

$Study$ $Break!$ Of college students between the ages 18 to 24, 97,000 have reported an alcohol related sexual assault.[26]

All too often, girls are left with a funny feeling the morning after a sexual encounter. They're left knowing that they didn't quite say yes, but that they didn't say no either. They might not even remember if they said yes or no, maybe from a roofie or maybe just because they had one too many beers but that guy took them home anyway.

---

25. RAINN, 2016
26. NIAAA, n.d.

It's important for everyone to understand the concept of consent, which is defined as "an agreement between participants to engage in sexual activity."[27] There are a lot of misconceptions about consent, and a lot of confusion too, but it comes down to communication. Partners should be communicating with one another throughout the entire sexual activity and in every subsequent one as well. The Rape, Abuse & Incest National Network (RAINN) says on their website that "giving consent for one activity, one time, does not mean giving consent for increased or recurring sexual contact. For example, agreeing to kiss someone doesn't give that person permission to remove your clothes. Having sex with someone in the past doesn't give that person permission to have sex with you again in the future... you can withdraw consent at any time.[28]"

Every sexual assault survivor's story is different, but that doesn't make one individual's story more powerful than another's. The trauma, the confusion, and the guilt can all wreck havoc on the individual and their life.

If this happens to you: it's not your fault. If it happens to your best friend, sister, or a random girl from your class: it's not their fault.

Your university has a counseling center and professionals who are trained to help sexual assault survivors. If you or your friend don't feel comfortable going in person, there are also national resources available.

Hotlines:

- **National Sexual Assault Telephone Hotline:** (800) 656-4673
- **Take Back the Night Foundation:** (866) 966-9013

---

27. RAINN, 2016
28. RAINN, 2016

Websites:

- **National Sexual Violence Resource Center** - http://www.nsvrc.org/

- **National Organization for Victim Assistance** - http://www.trynova.org/

- **Know Your IX** - https://www.knowyourix.org/

- **End Rape on Campus** - http://endrapeoncampus.org/

- **Take Back the Night Foundation** - https://takebackthenight.org/about-us/

Remember: you aren't alone and your family and friends will love and support you.

Speaking of family, I bet they would be proud, you took a minute to read about the serious stuff. Now let's look at all the fun ways your family can make college life easier for you.

Chapter 7

Home Sweet Home

I t'll be weird going home for the first time. You've been living on your own, practically an adult, and now you're expected to obey your parents' rules and be a teenager again? Hate to break it to you, but yes. Chances are, they still help pay your tuition. Plus we've all heard the cliché: my house, my rules.

It won't be too bad though. Your parents will be glad to have you home, even if it's just for the weekend. They've probably been empty nesting away in your absence. As time goes on, they'll adjust to their baby growing up, and you'll start to appreciate your parents more as the almost-adult that you are.

Just make sure you actually go home sometimes, even if it's just for the weekend.

Weekend at Bernie's, er Mom's

Maybe you're homesick 24/7, haven't settled into the routine of college life, and are constantly calling your mom and Facetiming your dog. Or maybe you've thrown yourself into involvement and your classes, are constantly going on ice cream runs with your floormates, and can't ever seem to find time to call your mom back — or to at least text her that you're still alive! No matter which situation you find yourself in, it's important that you find a balance with weekend visits.

For my homesick homies — jeeze, just typing that made me feel old and out of touch — college has an adjustment time. It's normal that you feel homesick. I promise, even the most involved and vivacious person on your floor has bouts of homesickness — they just might be better at hiding it. Remember, everyone here is new and everyone is going through the same experiences together. Make sure you don't go home too much, especially in the very beginning. While I don't want to say that if you don't make friends at the beginning, you won't make friends at all — that's just not true; you'll make friends throughout your entire college experience — but it will be harder. There's nothing worse than trying to break into an already-established friend group.

All right, now for you, college champs — I have to keep up my lame, post-grad persona, okay — I know you're having the time of your life and enjoying all that college has to offer, but remember your families (annoying siblings and overbearing parents included). Your families are proud of you, but that doesn't mean they aren't worried about you. Like I said earlier, make sure to check in occasionally, even if it's just a quick text. On that same note, try and go home. There will be at least one weekend not jam-packed with football games, retreats, or studying. You might find you even like being home sometimes.

You'll get to spend time with family and friends, eat a home-cooked meal, and most importantly, can bring home all your dirty laundry for Mom and Dad. There's a reason this stereotype exists — dorm washing machines leave a lot to be desired, and there's nothing worse than lugging three-weeks-worth of laundry up and down four flights of stairs.

Your parents will be glad to have you — and your laundry — home for the weekend. Make sure you spend some quality time with them, even if it's just watching a movie.

Obviously for all you out-of-staters, weekend visits are usually a no-go. Holiday breaks, however, you'll have to ~~suffer~~ behave just like everyone else — I kid, I kid. You'll appreciate your time at home during the holiday season even more.

Home for the Holidays

Most college students will spend the holidays at home. Not only are most school breaks scheduled around the holidays, but these are also the best times to visit your family and friends. If your parents are divorced, you may want to schedule which holidays you will spend with which parent. Having a schedule in advance will help avoid hurt feelings or misunderstandings later on.

The biggest difference between most weekend visits and holiday trips home? The length of time. Going home for a weekend is one thing — it's usually full of errands like haircuts and shopping that you just can't ever seem to find the time for while at school. You don't have time to be bored, and you're just grateful for free, home-cooked food.

That month-long winter break will start to lose some of its appeal when you're on day nine of a Netflix binge and have forgotten that the sky is blue. There are things you can do to alleviate the boredom that don't include paper writing or project doing, and some of them don't even require other people.

I'm sure there are things that you keep saying you'll do, but then life gets in the way. You've been telling yourself since tenth grade that one day you'd actually read *Pride and Prejudice* instead of just watching the movie, or maybe you've been wanting to start a journal. Use this break from school to start a project you've been putting off — I know you have the time.

Peer Perception: Alexandra Skidmore
Birmingham Southern College sophomore

The first time I came home from college it was confusing. I had spent the past two months away at school making my own decisions about where and when I did things. I expected that my parents would just automatically respect that and treat me the same way my college professors did. As a result, the first time I came home I found myself thinking things along the lines of "What do you mean I have a curfew?... It's 11:30 — why are you telling me to go to bed?... What do you mean I can't stay over at my friend's house?... Why are you telling me I can't have two desserts? I'm an adult; I can get my own food."

However, as the year went on, I realized that I had changed while I was away at school. I'd grown up and gotten used to doing things my own way. But my parents didn't know that. To them I was still their baby girl and they wanted to make sure I was safe. My 'I've got this' attitude was as strange and scary to them as their rules and control were frustrating to me. As annoying as it is, it's important to think about things from their point of view too.

I also realized that just because I didn't need to tell my parents about something while I was at school, that didn't mean I shouldn't tell them about it while I was at home. When I made plans I started asking myself, "Would I ask/tell my roommate before doing this?" My parents don't necessarily need to have any say over small things like what I had for dessert, or when I went to bed, but they certainly deserve to know what time I'm going to be home at night. or if I've invited people over. Those are things that affect them, because they live in the house, too, and they'll worry if I'm not home on time.

It can be hard to find things to do over long breaks as well. The first few days are really exciting because you're seeing all your family, and you have stories to tell from college and they have stories to tell about what's happened while you were away. However, odds are that your parents have jobs and you'll go stir crazy after a few days at home. It can be good to find reasons to get out of the house. Try to meet up with some of your friends from high school, go for a walk in the park, visit your favorite restaurants. If your break is long enough you can even try to get a job. Even if you're one of the lucky few who don't need the money, having a job can be a good way to get out of the house for a few hours a day and interact with other people. I know it sounds a lot like something your mom would suggest, but it can also be good to go visit your grandparents while you're home. They're just as eager to see you and hear all about your time at college, and they're probably less busy than the rest of your family.

Eventually though, you'll want to leave the house. Plan fun outings for your family. Your parents and siblings will be happy that you want to spend time with them. especially after all those angsty teen years when you weren't exactly pleasant to be around (it's okay — we all were). Look up day trips near your hometown or suggest going out for dinner at new restaurant.

If an outing isn't possible because both your parents work full-time, make them dinner or a special dessert. You've probably forgotten what it's like to live in a house with a fully-stocked kitchen, so familiarize yourself again. You might even get to leave the house for groceries — and you really do need a break from that computer screen.

Make plans with your old high school friends too. Just because you may have drifted apart during the semester while you were all at different schools doesn't mean the friendship isn't still alive and well. Everyone will have new experiences and stories to tell.

If possible, try to get a job during this break. While the time constraints may not make it feasible, check with your old job to see if they need any extra help during the holiday season or fully embrace the high school life-style by getting your old babysitting gig back. It's also a good idea to see if anyone in your neighborhood or your parents' friends need a pet walker or a house sitter. Many people leave for the holiday season, leaving their houses and pets untended. No matter how you do it, you'll appreciate the extra cash when you're back at school.

Care Packages

Sometimes home can come to you. While no where near as satisfying as actually going home for some home-cooked meals and free snacks, care packages can help ease the homesickness in between visits.

Whether they include letters from home, your mom's famous chocolate chip cookies, or drawings from younger siblings, care packages offer an excellent connection to home. When stress levels are high because of finals or roommate issues, care packages can brighten your day like nothing else.

Print out labels with your dorm address and leave them at home for your mom and dad to easily mail out packages. Talk with them about what you would most like to see in a care package and even write a list of your favorite items — they may love you, but that doesn't mean they remember which kid loves Twizzlers and which one M&Ms.

While the best care packages are personalized to you, here's a list of some general care package ideas:

- Mom's homemade cookies (not only will you love them, but your roommate will love you for sharing them)

- Handwritten notes from family

- Pictures of your pets

- Your favorite author's latest book

- Magazines

- Your local newspaper

- Healthy snack foods (Be sure to include some healthy options like popcorn, and not the extra butter kind. With late-night studying in your future, you will want some munchies, but you do not want your care package to add to your waistline.)

- Special toiletry items — items that only a local shop sells or that might be a little too pricey for your college freshman budget

- Themed holiday boxes with candy and decorations for your dorm room door

- Starbucks gift cards

- Coffee beans and/or K-cups

Whether you get to go home as frequently as you like or care packages are your only connection to home during the semester, enjoy the time that you have there. College can be stressful and exhausting, so home will be a much-needed break. Plus, you'll get your laundry done for free!

Speaking of free, how exactly do you plan on paying for all of your college expenses? Don't worry — I've got you covered in the next chapter.

Chapter 8

Finding Finances

F unding college is stressful for most students. Not only do you have to pay tuition and room and board, but there are additional expenses like books, access codes, planners, school supplies, and computers. It seems like college life eats your money, doesn't it? I mean that literally. Those late-night pizza runs can really start to add up. Plus, if you're anything like me, you also have to consider how much money you'll inevitably spend on coffee. I'd rather not divulge how much of my hard-earned money has ended up at Starbucks, Dunkin, or my favorite local coffee shop, but let's just say it was a lot.

Plus, you've gotta have fun while in school too, and unfortunately many fun activities usually require money.

Depending on your situation, you might be trying to hold down a job while you are a student. Some students choose to work part-time to have some extra spending money, while others need the extra money to pay for their living expenses. A lot of students might even have to work full-time to support themselves because their family can't help. Whatever your situation, there are some things you should know before deciding to take a job as a student that will help you juggle all the responsibilities that come with college life.

Before getting a job, weigh the pros and cons of working while a student. Your time will already be overtaxed with class, studying, involvement, and trying to maintain a social life. If your situation allows, try to avoid working during your first semester. This will allow you to get acclimated to college life and know your schedule so that you can determine how much time you have to work.

If you decide getting a part-time job is what you want to do or have to do to finance your college career, consider all your options: work study programs, internships, retail, food service, nannying; the possibilities are endless.

Job Hunting

There's a lot to consider when looking for a job, which leaves the job possibilities almost endless depending on your needs and interests.

Some key things to consider:

> **Work-Study** Are you eligible for work-study? Work-study is a federally-funded program that provides job opportunities through the university based on financial need. To find out if you qualify, inquire with your financial aid office. Jobs tend to be on-campus office work and you'll be paid hourly.[29]

> **On-campus vs Off-campus** Do you want to work on- or off-campus? On-campus jobs can range from office work and being a teacher's assistant to food service and catering waiter. The biggest perk of on-campus job opportunities is that they're

---

29. FAFSA, 2017

largely targeted at students, so they will be flexible and make your schedule around classes and holiday breaks. Off-campus jobs usually have more variety and positions available since they cater to the town as the whole, not just campus residents and faculty. This also opens up possibilities like nannying.

Transportation It's important to think about how you'll get to your new place of employment. Is it within walking distance? If not, do you have access to a car or will you be taking the bus? Are buses reliable in your college town? Reliable transportation can determine whether you're able to take a job or not, so don't forget to think about it.

Study Break! In the past 25 years, more than 70 percent of students have held a job while in college.[30]

OK, so you've decided what kind of jobs you want. How do you go about finding open positions? While your parents may tell you to "hit the pavement" and show up to local businesses with resumes, businesses are increasingly using the internet to post job openings. When I was looking for my first job, at least half of the businesses I went to told me to just apply for the job online — I wasted a perfectly good day's makeup! If the business is corporately owned, their website will most likely have a "career" section where you'll input location information before being redirected to the application. Check Monster, Indeed, and Craigslist for local job openings. It's also worthwhile to let your friends and acquaintances know that you're looking for a job. They may know of someone who is hiring or even be able to put in a good word for you at their job.

---

30. Rapacon, 2015.

Interesting Internships

Internships are a great employment opportunity that many freshmen don't think about — that's a problem for junior or senior you, right? Wrong. While many internships do require students to be an upperclassman, many others don't. Go to your college's career fair — a lot of the employers present will be local businesses looking for part-time interns. Even if you aren't able to land an internship your freshman year, you'll have a leg up on all the other freshman who don't even know where the career resource center is.

Internships often offer college students valuable experience that help students get a job after college. Some internships pay fairly well, while others pay little or no money at all. If they don't pay well, that doesn't mean you should immediately discount them. A lot of majors require that students take an internship for credit, so it can still be beneficial to you.

Ask your college counselor about these opportunities. If you know a company that you would like to work for after college, contact them directly about internship programs they offer. Internships will give you an advantage once you graduate college over students that have no experience. If you know your major and already know the field you want to work in when you graduate, an internship can be a solid addition to your resume. You might even find a full-time job waiting for you at the same place you interned when you graduate.

Unique opportunities

There are a lot of ways to earn money that many students don't think about that give all the flexibility a college student needs. If you're interested in editing and writing, consider becoming a freelance editor or writer.

Peer Perception: Jessica Piper

I started getting paid to write when I was 18.

Working as a freelance writer allows me to do my work on my own time. While I have to keep to my deadlines, I do my job when it's convenient for me — for example, when I am traveling or on days where I don't have too much other work, as I am still a college student. Before I began writing, I worked at a café, with the same long shifts every Saturday and Sunday, which didn't give me much free time as a full-time student. I like having the freedom to fit my work to my schedule.

She encourages young writers to make sure they are OK with the level of compensation they are receiving for their service. "Especially when you are young, people may try to pay you very little or take advantage of you in other ways," she says."In the writing world, many places ask you to write but won't pay you — they say you benefit from the 'exposure.' If you are starting your own business, you probably want to get paid. Make sure you are working with people who recognize this goal and value your time and energy."

If you're more the type of person to ace your calculus or bio exam, consider being a tutor. There will be plenty of your classmates that need the extra help or you can tutor high schoolers in the area — I know, it's weird to think about people just living their lives in your college town!

Maybe you're really good at painting or are always crafting away. Consider selling your work, either on Etsy or to your friends and family. While this won't be a source of steady cash, it'll be a fun way for you to earn some extra cash in your free time — and you'll actually enjoy it, unlike hour six at a fast food restaurant.

No matter what job you decide on, it's important that you talk to your manager about your responsibilities as a student. Be honest and straightforward about the time commitment you'll be able to guarantee and request time off around midterms and finals — I know you have the dates written in your planner somewhere! He or she will appreciate the responsibility and concern for the company and your co-workers by ensuring that someone will be able to cover your shift ahead of time.

Working while in college is part of the experience, but remember that school must come first. To help offset the pressure, apply for as many scholarships and grants as you can.

Searching for Scholarships and Grants

The National Center for Education Statistics reports that there are 750,000 scholarships available, equaling $1.2 billion.[31] While it's nice to know that scholarship money is out there, it can be overwhelming to start searching for and applying for scholarships, especially when senior year is already so busy. As consuming as it is, it's important to apply to scholarships, and as

---

31. Geary, 2002

many of them as you can. It's a myth that only the very active and top-of-the-class can win scholarships, because with over 750,000 available, that's not the case. While merit-based scholarships do make up a chunk of available scholarships (you should apply to those if you qualify), they are not the only ones available. The main categories of scholarships are:

- Merit-based: based on academic achievements, including grades and standardized test scores

- Need-based: if your family's income falls below a certain threshold (which varies per scholarship)

- Community service: those hours spent at the humane society can really pay off

- First in family: available to students who are the first in their family to attend college

- Writing scholarships: different than required essays for many scholarships, these are based solely on an individual's writing ability

Study Break! Two-thirds of full time college students used financial aid to help pay for college in the 2014-2015 school year.[32]

Other than scholarships, there are often many grants available as well. These are typically from the state or federal government. These can be either need- or merit-based, and typically only require the FAFSA, Federal Application for Student Aid, to be completed — more on that later. Some states offer aid that covers all or part of your tuition, if you meet the qual-

---

32. Big Future, n.d.

ifications. These grants and their requirements vary state by state, so double check with your guidance counselor and online.

Peer Perception: *Kristen Joseph*
University of Chicago sophomore

When I began my college search, the two main things that I judged every option against were affordability and ambiance. My parents are far from wealthy, and while they took amazing care of me and my siblings, they were never able to save up any extra money for college expenses. I had a job and continually applied to different scholarships, but the prospect of not being able to afford college was still worrisome. So naturally, I wanted to go to a school that would offer me enough financial aid to cover almost all of my expenses. And, with any luck, that school would have a campus culture that I felt comfortable in (and buildings that looked similar to the Hogwarts castle in Harry Potter, because I have a penchant for gothic architecture).

Fast-forward to college acceptance letter season. I had applied to six schools, and had gotten into most of them, but I was still waiting on the status of my application at my dream school, the University of Chicago. With a gorgeous campus, delightfully quirky culture, top tier academics, and proximity to a major city, this school had it all. The only problem: I didn't think they would accept me. Sure, I was in the top 10 percent of my graduating class academically, but UChicago only accepts the top 7 percent of applicants in the entire nation! Not to mention the fact that the price tag on this school was the most expensive that I had seen anywhere, with an equivalent cost for both in-state and out-of-state students.

I had already resigned myself to the belief that I wouldn't be going there — even if I did receive an acceptance letter from UChicago, there was no way I would be able to afford the cost of attendance... so you can imagine my surprise when I not only received an acceptance letter from the University of Chicago, but also a financial aid package that covered the complete cost of attendance without making me take out any loans!

I was shocked, but also very excited. I would be able to afford my dream school! I still took out a very small loan to cover out-of-pocket costs like non-dining-hall food and flights back home during breaks. My family and I did the 16-hour drive from Florida to Chicago, Illinois, for my orientation weekend. I'm glad we got there safely, but I never want to drive that route again; we encountered everything from flat tires to highways riddled with potholes on the way up, so you can trust me when I say that flying is a much better option if you live more than a couple hours' drive from your school. It's also very important to make sure that you have weather-appropriate clothing. For example, the Midwest winters are actually bearable for this Florida girl because of puffy coats, winter boots, warm hats, and thick leggings under my jeans.

All in all, I'm very happy with where I ended up. The campus is beautiful, the academics are adequately challenging, and I've made some great friends and definitely feel like I belong there. I never thought I'd be able to go to the University of Chicago, yet here I am today. I guess that just goes to show that attending your dream school is actually an attainable goal.

It's important that you don't stop applying for scholarships after your college acceptance. Many times there are scholarships only available to students with a specific declared major or who has shown dedication to a club during the college years. If you do decide to go Greek, many fraternities and sororities offer scholarships, both need- and merit-based.

Banks and Budgets

Earning — and budgeting — your money is an important skill. For a lot of college students, this will be the first time they've had to be responsible for a budget larger than their monthly allowance or summer job fund. Budgeting, like anything else, takes practice.

The Bare Necessities

Before you can really start controlling your money, you need to build a foundation. Do you have a bank account set up? A credit card? Do you even own a checkbook?

Let's assume that you don't have a checking or savings account. Maybe you've never even set foot inside a bank before. That's all about to change. It's important that you have an account set up.

Checking accounts rarely earn interest, or earn little interest. Savings accounts, on the other hand, more often than not earn a higher interest rate. Most people will have both a savings and checking account. The savings account should be used to save money for big purchases or long-term goals. The checking account is useful for buying smaller items and paying bills on a monthly basis. You can open savings and checking accounts with the same bank or different banks. If you have both accounts with the same bank, it might be easier to transfer money back and forth, if that is something you will need to do often. Even if you have different banks for your checking and savings accounts, you will be able to transfer money back and forth between the two accounts. Different banks might just take longer to complete the transfer.

When you open an account, whether checking or savings accounts, be sure to read the fine print. Ask about additional charges and fees. Some banks limit the number of transactions you can make a month. Some banks may have a minimum balance requirement and will charge you monthly fees if your balance drops below the minimum. Find out upfront about the fees your bank might charge you. Ask about different account options. Most banks offer a few different types of checking accounts, and chances are there will be a "student" account option. If you are not carrying a large balance, ask about a "free" checking account. Often these accounts will not limit the number of transactions you can have a month without charging you fees.

When you open your account, you'll get a debit card, or check card. This card can be used as an ATM card but also carries a credit card logo, normally a Visa or MasterCard symbol. This cards can be swiped as a debit card, where you enter your ATM pin on the keypad, or can be used like a credit card without entering your pin. Bear in mind that no matter which option you choose when using this card, the money will be drafted from your checking account. If you do not have the money in your account to pay for your purchase, do not buy it. Most banks offer overdraft protection, which allow the payment to process, but you'll be left with large fees. Suddenly your $3 coffee is now a $43 coffee — not worth it, even to my coffee-addicted self.

Credit cards are a bit trickier. College students are often flooded with credit card offers, which can be overwhelming. What's the difference between

Discover card and a credit card from your bank? Should you have more than one?

Credit cards allow you to purchase items now, on credit, and pay for them later. Most cards come with a certain grace period, usually around a month, to pay off the balance in full with no additional interest. If you do not pay your balance in full each month, you will be paying interest on your total balance. In essence, you will be paying more than sticker price for the items you purchased earlier.

As a college student, credit cards should be used for only two reasons: emergencies and to build credit. Emergency situations include your car breaking down on the side of the road and having to tow it to a mechanic or a late night visit to the emergency room — not if you don't have the cash to buy tickets to see Beyoncé. If you use your credit card too freely, you might wake up to find yourself in more credit card debt than from your student loans — and trust me, you will have enough of those.

Building credit is an important reason to have a credit card, however. If you use your card for small purchases and keep track of what you spend to make sure you can pay it off at the end of the month, you will start building a credit history. Banks and loan officers use credit scores to determine whether to grant a car or house loan and the interest rate. It's important to start building good credit early — much like your GPA, it's easy to tank your credit score, but much harder to rebuild it.

If you decide to get a credit card, it's important to do research beforehand — shop around, so to speak. Read the terms and conditions to find out what interest rate the card is charging you, just in case you ever have to run a balance on the card. Check to see if there is an annual fee for having the card. You should be able to find a card with a reasonable interest rate and no annual fee, even as a college student. Many cards also offer rewards programs. Some of these programs offer airline miles, cash back, or other discounts and benefits. Be sure to read through the terms of rewards cards. Commonly, the rewards are not as good as the initial offer make them out to be. Do not feel limited by just the offers you receive in the mail. Check online for other offers. Many websites compare offers from several different credit card companies.

Budgeting

The easiest way to manage your money: creating a budget. The hardest part of managing your money: sticking to your budget.

If you are not an accounting major or numbers make you nervous, do not freak out. Budgeting does not require an in-depth knowledge of economics or accounting. Actually, budgeting is quite simple: spend less than you bring in. If you spend more than you bring in, your budget will bust. If you are not technically making money, your budget might be to spend less than your parents or financial aid gives you. Creating a simple budget should be doable for most college students.

To begin a budget, make a list of areas that you will be spending money on: tuition, room and board, car expenses (gas, insurance, maintenance), entertainment, eating out, school supplies, laundry, toiletries, and clothes.

Next, list your income, including a part-time job and an allowance from your parents. Go through your list of expenses and estimate how much a money you will spend on each area. Add up your total estimate expenses then subtract the total expenses from your total income. If you have a negative number, your budget needs to be adjusted. Go back through your expenses and start cutting until you reach a positive number. If you leave a cushion, you will have room for unexpected expenses. When creating your expense list, be sure to include a savings or rainy day fund. You never know when you will have an unexpected car repair or want to spend extra one month on entertainment when your favorite band comes to town.

Your original budget might need to be amended once you implement it. You might find you spend less on gas and more on food than you originally planned. If you are having trouble guessing how much you will spend each month on expenses, take a month to keep track of all your purchases. Get a small notebook that you can carry around with you or make a note on your phone. Each time you spend money, whether getting a soda from a machine or buying gas for your car, write it down. At the end of the month, add up how much you spent on each area and use that as a guide for your budget. There are apps that do this as well, like Mint, but I find that I'm more conscious of my spending when I keep track of it manually.

If your parents are good at budgeting (and not all parents are), ask them to help you create your budget. Your school might offer a class on budgeting as well. Check into what your college offers in the way of help for keeping ahead of your finances.

It's important that you create healthy spending habits while in college. It will help your meager funds last longer and hopefully prevent you from drowning in debt upon graduation.

Debt: The Debbie Downer of Adulthood

Sometimes debt is inevitable. Maybe the tires on your car finally gave out and you had to charge the new ones on your brand new credit or maybe you had to take out student loans to afford tuition. Debt isn't always avoidable, but there are smart ways of managing your debt that will allow you to pay it off quickly — and save yourself money in the process.

Study Break!   Graduating with some debt is normal, 73 percent of 2017 college graduates finished school with some form of debt.[33]

Credit cards

As I previously mentioned, credit cards are one of the basic essentials when it comes to financial planning. They allow you to build credit — so long as you responsibly pay them back. Having a credit card often feels like free money, but that kind of mindset is what gets people into thousands of dollars of debt. It's easy to swipe and swipe when you don't see your bank account dwindling, but then the bill comes and you don't have enough money to pay.

On your statement, there will be two numbers listed: the account balance in full and the minimum payment required to avoid late fees and a drop in your credit score. Even if you can't pay the full balance, it's imperative that you pay

---

33. Fay, 2017.

the minimum balance. If you can manage, it's best if you pay as much of the balance off as you can. If not, your balance will accrue interest.

An interest rate, or an annual percentage rate (ARP), is the cost of borrowing money — and how credit cards and banks make money. The credit card company Discover uses the analogy of miles per hour to explain what ARP is:

> "just like 'miles per hour' is a way of measuring speed over an hour, APR measures interest over the time period of a year. But in both cases, the measurement can still be used for longer or shorter time periods.[34]"

The ARP can range, and a lot of companies even waive them the first year — don't be fooled by this, and read the fine print.

So how exactly does the ARP work? If you have an APR of 15 percent, the daily rate is .041096 percent[35]. If you have a balance of $400 on your credit card from groceries and gas — which you have an allowance for — and that North Face jacket you just couldn't live without, but can only pay $150 off the balance, you will have a remainder of $250. Once that rolls over to the next month, interest on the payment will be $1.23. While that may seem like a negligible amount, that's money that you are essentially giving away and it can easily add up as you accrue more and more debt.

It's important that if you're going to use a credit card that you do so responsibly and keep your balance low and your credit score high, or you might find yourself regretting that North Face jacket purchase.

---

34. Discover, n.d.
35. Discover, n.d.

Tips for keeping credit card debt low:

- Minimize the amount of cards you open. It can be hard to keep track of multiple cards with multiple balances, so keep life simple by only have one or two credit cards active at any time.

- Only use your card for necessities like gas and groceries. If you only spend money on items you have to purchase and are included in your budget already, you'll have the money to pay off your balance on payday.

- Set up automatic payments for the minimum payment. While ideally you'll be paying off your balance in full every month, this will at least prevent any additional late fees from being incurred.

- Don't use one credit card to pay off another. With this method, you're essentially paying interest on top of interest. Just do your best to make the minimums on both cards while focusing on paying one card off in full.

I know it's tempting to use credit cards to pay for everything, but be careful. Most students are already in thousands of dollars of student loan debt by the time they graduate, so there's no need to add credit card debt to the mix as well.

Student loans

According to CNN, the average college graduate is $27,000 in debt.[36] While it may only be your first year of college, that doesn't mean you shouldn't be thinking about the future — remember those plans and goals?

---

36. Ellis, 2012

Study Break!   The average payment plan for student loans lasts 20-25 years. Sometimes borrowers qualify for a forgiveness plan if payments are made on time for a set amount of years.[37]

Ideally you'll have summer jobs and internships that allow you to pay for what your parents can't cover, but sometimes student loans are unavoidable. It may be that you don't have time to work and make the grades you need for graduation or maybe it's the only way you can pay for that summer session in Australia. Graduating with student loan debt is common and thousands before you have been able to pay off their debt with their high paying jobs post-graduation — that is why you decided on college, right?

By this point, you're probably already familiar with the FAFSA and the Federal Student Aid website — you've gotta be if you've received any federal student loans. This page is where you'll go for exit counseling and any other questions you might have about paying your loans back, including a payment estimate calculator based on your income post-graduation, amount of debt you've accumulated, and the interest rate.

Types of Loans

Student loans are already confusing enough, but there are multiple types of loans that you can take out as a student. Any loan administered by the federal government is a federal loan — these are the loans that require the FAFSA application. They typically have lower interest rates than private loans and are included with your financial aid package.[38]

---

37. Fay, 2017.
38. Federal Student Aid, 2017

There are two main subsections of federal loans:

- Federal Perkins Loan Program: A school-based loan program reserved for students who demonstrate "exceptional" financial need. Under this program, the school is the lender.

- William D. Ford Federal Direct Loan Program: This is the largest federal student loan program; The Department of Education is the lender. There are four kinds of loans that fall under this program:

  - Direct Subsidized loans: available for undergraduate students who need assistance with covering the cost of higher education

  - Direct Unsubsidized Loans: available to undergraduate, graduate, and professional students; student does not have to demonstrate financial need

  - Direct PLUS Loans: available to graduate or professional students and parents of dependent undergraduate students

  - Direct Consolidation Loans: available to all students and allows individual to combine all eligible student loan to make payment easier[39]

Talk to your financial aid advisor and your parents before making any decisions about whether to take out loans or how much to borrow. It's a big decision, and it's better to have the opinions of people older and more experienced than you to help you decide.

One way or another, you'll figure out how to finance not only your first year of college, but the next three as well.

---

39. Federal Student Aid, 2017

Chapter 9

Getting to Graduation

Image a fine spring day. The sun is shining brightly; a gentle breeze rustles the lush, green grass under your feet. The day seems perfect and as you look around, you see your family and friends all watching you, smiling proudly. Your name is called and you stand and walk across the stage — or dance like many of my fellow graduates. You are handed your diploma, a symbol of the hard work and dedication that you have worked the last four years to get. As you pose for a picture at the end of the stage, your mind flashes back to all the good times you have been through while you were in college. You recall the friends you made, the late-night study sessions, the parties, the laughs, the cramped dorm rooms, the once-white-but-now-pink shirts from your first attempt at laundry on your own. You think back to all of it — the times you thought you would never make it through and the times you knew you could make it. And somehow, all of it now seems worth it. All the challenges you went through seem to have added something valuable to this piece of paper you now hold in your hands. Also, you realize as you close this one door, so many more will be opening.

Your graduation day, even if it rains or you trip walking across the stage, will feel amazing. You will be proud of yourself and you will know that your family and friends are proud of you too. My own graduation was nothing like the above scenario. I graduated from the University of Florida, so by late April there was no such thing as a "fine spring day." Our ceremony was fairly short: the president spoke, they read the names, we walked across the stage, and didn't even get a placeholder for our diploma — that would be mailed to us later. I could not find my family in the crowd and they mispronounced my last name when they called me to get my degree.

Despite all that, my graduation day was one of the happiest, proudest days of my life. Looking back, I would not trade it for the world.

Big Picture: Taking a Step Back

As you journey through college, while it's important to stay focused on your goal, bear in mind that college is a marathon. You do not have to win every leg of the race; you just have to keep going. You just have to make it to the finish line. Whatever pitfalls you might face or road blocks you come across, keep going. Do not let anything or anyone keep you from graduation.

Learning is truly a lifelong process. Learn about history, the world around you, other cultures, your own culture, yourself, relationships, laundry, driving a stick-shift car, and everything else you can learn. Be thirsty for knowledge and continually seek ways to quench that thirst. Be a positive inspiration to your friends and classmates and help them realize the value of learning too.

It's easy to get bogged down by papers, tests, and applications and forget that you're supposed to be enjoying your college experience as well. Many people say their college years were the best times of their lives. As you go through your college years, you may not always believe that to be true, but do not forget that someday you'll look back and think fondly of your time in school. Take tons of pictures. Make scrapbooks of you and your friends to help recall those times once you are out of school. Have your friends write notes about what they recall of a certain event and keep those notes in your scrapbook. Keep concert ticket stubs and football tickets — even from the season it seemed like your team forgot how to play — I did say I went to the University of Florida. 2013 was a rough year for Gator football, but that doesn't mean the games weren't fun. Keep all the little things that mean something to you. One day, those little pieces of memories will mean the world to you.

Job Shadowing and Internships

It's important to remember what you're coming to college for: getting an education that will enable you to find your dream job and lead a fulfilling career. Before you can get that far, you've got to figure out just what it is exactly that you want to do.

Study Break!   65 percent of the 2015 Bachelor's degree graduating class were students who took on at least one internship before graduating.[40]

Internships and job shadowing give you a glimpse into the career you think you want. My first internship was as a marketing intern at a publishing company in a field I wasn't all that interested in. By the end of the first semester, I knew that while the publishing industry was still the goal, I no longer wanted to work in marketing and advertising; I wanted to work in editorial. I also fell in love with a genre I'd never expected, which opened up hundreds of more possibilities for a job post-graduation.

So you know the importance of internships, but how do you get them? You're asking the same question as every other college kid out there.

Your university most likely has a career resource center — and they probably have a website — that will give you information on upcoming career days and job fairs, crafting the perfect resume and cover letter, and job interview tips. Your college/department will likely have something similar, only centric to your major; there are definitely differences for an engineer's resume verses a graphic designer's. Along with general tips, many college career centers post job listings for any openings that they hear about.

Even though you're only a freshman, it's never too early to start getting resume critiques and to attend career fairs. Like anything else, interviewing takes time and practice before you'll have mastered the art. It's important to get that practice in while getting an internship would be ideal, not when it's critical.

---

40. Dobbs, 2016.

Andrea Bronstein
University of Florida graduate

Exactly two years ago today, I submitted my first applications for a summer internship. As many other juniors in college, I felt that I had to get an internship for the summer before senior year in order to become competitive for the job market.

A little background on myself at this time: I was studying advertising with a business concentration and had a 3.5 GPA. My previous work experience included working in a restaurant in high school, an advertising sales internship with the Independent Florida Alligator, an Operations Supervisor position at the University of Florida's RecSports, and a brand ambassador position with Amazon and 5-hour ENERGY. I worked several jobs concurrently while attending a great university. Needless to say, I wasn't worried about finding an internship.

As the months and applications continued to progress, I began to get much more worried. After eight months and over 150 applications, I felt defeated and took a position at a local online marketing agency in Gainesville. I watched many people I know relocate for the summer and work for many Fortune 500 companies I interviewed with. I interviewed with 20 companies and went through several rounds of interviews each with these companies. After each rejection I sought feedback and was pretty much told, "There was nothing wrong with you, we just went with someone better."

I was devastated, but nonetheless I worked hard at my local job and learned about a fascinating industry. Although I wasn't traveling around the United States or living in a new place, I was able to learn about search engine optimization and other interesting facets of online marketing. I also learned for myself, that I was no longer interested in a marketing role, but more interested in sales and being in the field and out of an office every day.

The September of my senior year, I hit the floor running even harder. I precisely edited every application and cover letter. By November, I received three job offers, including my first choice position. Although I didn't have a fancy internship on my resume, I was very transparent with these companies and proved to them I was willing to work hard and would be a great asset for them. For my final on-site interview for my current job, I spent hours learning all about the company/industry and prepared insightful questions while others showed up unprepared. In the end, I was chosen over many other students who had interned at top companies because I showed an eagerness to learn and competitive drive. Finding an internship and job is very difficult, but don't give up or settle.

Andrea Bronstein is a recent graduate of the University of Florida. She currently works for Anheuser-Busch as a Sales Trainee.

The Possibility of Studying Abroad

Studying abroad. It sounds so grown up and sophisticated doesn't it? Could you think of a better way to spend a semester than traipsing around Paris, eating cheese and bread for every meal, or exploring the Mayan ruins in Guatemala — almost doesn't feel like there should be any studying happening, does there?

Well, studying abroad isn't as much of an impossibility as you might think. In fact, in 2014 alone over 300,000 students studied abroad and received academic credit for doing so.[41] Most universities have a partnership with schools to make it easier for students. These partnership programs typically last for a full academic semester. Students are usually on their own for finding lodging, although there are resources available to assist them, and take classes directly at the university. With these programs, some measure of fluency is ideal, although many universities, especially partner schools, offer classes in English at well.

41. USA Study Abroad, 2017

Study Break! Companies look highly upon study abroad experiences, especially for business majors, as 40 percent of businesses admitted to missed opportunities because their employees lacked the international negotiation skills.[42]

Another option available is school-sponsored trips. These are usually shorter, only for a summer semester, which is typically six to eight weeks. These groups are led by U.S. faculty and usually include the cost for lodging, along with tuition, in the upfront price.

Whichever route you take chances are it won't be expensive as you might think. Usually you'll end up paying tuition to your home school, and you'll have verification that the credits will transfer. If you do study abroad, make sure that you budget for all additional expenses. Transoceanic flights are expensive, and you'll probably end up spending more money on adventures and experiences than you would be stateside, as you should be.

42. NAFSA, n.d.

Setting Goals and Planning

In order to spend your summer traipsing around Roman ruins or as an intern at your dream company (hey Scholastic, are you hiring?), you have to set goals and make plans. Think waaaay back to Chapter 1. Remember those long-term and short-term goals you put together? College is when you start to work towards those goals and maybe even see some of them realized.

Set goals for each year of school. If you are thinking of studying abroad in your senior year or want to take on an internship by your junior year, write it down. Want to maintain a 3.0 GPA or better? Maybe you want to find a club you're passionate about. Or maybe you just want to take one class that's out of your comfort zone.

Whatever your goals are, write them down. At the beginning of each year, review the goals you set. Go back to your original mission statement for your college career and make any necessary changes. Setting goals early will help you be more successful in the long run. Do not get too upset if you do not accomplish all your goals. Recall the saying that if you aim for the stars and fall short, you still made it further than if you had set your sights lower. So go ahead and aim high.

To help yourself reach those goals, you've got to plan out your life — or at the very least, your week. There's nothing worse than realizing too late that you can't go to that show downtown with your friends because you forgot you had a paper due or going to the career fair unprepared because you didn't have time to update your resume.

Planning is more than just the day-to-day though. Just as you scheduled your freshman year classes before you started your first class, you should look ahead to your four years of school. Schedule your classes for all four years while you are still a freshman. Of course, you might change your mind about your classes and if your major changes, your schedule of classes will obviously change too. But having a schedule for all four years will help you see what classes you need to take at what time and help you more realistically manage your class schedule for your entire four years. If you do not plan ahead at all, you might find yourself as a senior taking freshman level classes that you missed. Do not count on your college advisors to take care of your scheduling for you. The counselors are there to assist you, but it is your responsibility to make sure you graduate on time.

Conclusion

The Next Three Years

As you go through the next three years, just remember that time flies when you're having fun. I know, I know: it's a cliché, but clichés are true for a reason, right?

College will go by more quickly than you can imagine, which is part of why those goals and plans are so important. Don't put off the necessary tasks that will allow you to fulfill your dreams, even when it sounds like a much better idea to binge-watch an entire season of something on Netflix. You're in college for a reason, so try to not get distracted. Future you will thank past you for not procrastinating (much) and for planning ahead.

That being said, enjoy the time that you have in college. You'll never again be in an environment so rich and diverse in what it offers you, and you'll never again be as carefree and young as you are in college. Be open to new experiences and to new people and mindsets, both in the classroom and out. Always wanted to take a class on obscure West African art? Do it. That's what college is for. You'll never again be granted the opportunity to take in the world around you as you are in college. You'll also never find yourself within walking distance of your best friends again, where spontaneous, late-night ice cream runs require no more planning than a text and movie nights can last well into the night with no thoughts about an early morning at work to put a damper on the fun.

You're only in college — well, undergrad — for four years of your life. Make the most of it. Appreciate it while you still can.

To quote the completely-impossible-to-see-but-still-amazing musical, Hamilton:

"Look around, look around, at how lucky we are to be alive right now."

Author's Note

When I was given the opportunity to write this book, I knew I was the perfect author. I'm a recent graduate from the University of Florida, a part of the Spring 2017 class — which if nothing else explains the large number of case studies from University of Florida students. I just got my freshly-minted adult card and can still remember what it's like to walk into that first class, terrified you're in the wrong building or that you accidentally enrolled in a third-year class (this actually happened to me my freshman fall semester — I immediately dropped the class.) I can remember the struggles of sorority recruitment at an SEC school in the middle of August (for all you girls thinking about rushing, bring flats, coffee filters to blot your face, and a whole lot of water).

All too often, books that are meant for a teen audience that are written by adults fail to hit their mark. While well-meaning, they lack the firsthand knowledge of what it's like to be a teenager and to go off to college in this decade. I've tried to be truthful and honest about what you'll expect, from homework to homesickness. College won't be easy, but there's a reason your uncle always brings up his college days at every family function: it's fun, it's challenging, and it's rewarding. Enjoy it.

Glossary

Admission: A student's acceptance for enrollment

Advisor: Counselor who offers academic advice to students

Bachelor's Degree: Awarded for a four-year degree, usually after 120 or 124 semester hours

Certificate: A document that verifies completion of a specific area of study

Class Schedule: When registering each semester, this document includes course details (when, where) and prerequisites.

Core requirements: More often than not, these classes are mandatory for all students of a school or university.

Course numbers: The numbers assigned to specific classes found in a college's catalog and used when registering for classes

Courses: Listed in a college's catalog, these are classes available to students. The catalog should list the course number, title, description, and units of credit the course is worth.

Credit hour: Credit given for attending one lecture hour of class each week for 15 weeks or equivalent. Most college classes are three credit hours.

Curriculum (program): Courses required for a specific degree or certificate.

Degree plan: A specific list of required courses and electives to be completed for a degree

Departments: Academic areas offering courses in one or more disciplines

Doctoral degree: The most advanced degree that can be earned

Drop and add: Changes made to a student's schedule. Check the academic calendar for the drop/add deadlines for each term to not be penalized.

Elective: Course available but not required for a specific field of study. Students can decide which elective classes they want to take.

FAFSA: The Free Application for Federal Student Aid is a form that can be filled out annually by current and incoming university students (both undergraduate and graduate) and sometimes their parents to determine their eligibility for federal student financial aid.

Fees: Course-related costs to attend college

Financial aid: Any financial assistance including scholarships, work-study jobs, or grants to eligible students

Freshman: A student who has completed less than 30 hours of college credit

Full-time student: An undergraduate student enrolled in 12 or more credit hours per semester

General Education requirement (Gen-eds): A group of courses required to earn a degree commonly required for all students in the same college or university

GPA: Grade point average; the average of your class grades, commonly based on a 4.0 scale

Grants: Financial assistance that does not require repayment

Greek Life: A term used to describe fraternity or sorority groups on campus

Internship: A job in a student's field of study, which might be required to earn degrees by some schools

Junior: A student who has completed 60 to 89 college credit hours

Loans: Financial assistance that must be repaid

Major: A concentration of courses in a specific area or a student's field of study

Master's degree: A graduate degree that normally requires two or more years of study beyond the bachelor's degree

Minor: A student's secondary field of study

Nonresident: A student who lives out of state or does not meet specific state residency requirements (more often than not, students must live in the state for at least a year before starting college to be considered a resident)

Online courses: Classes held on the internet

Part-time student: A student enrolled in less than 12 units in a semester

Prerequisite: A course that must be taken before enrollment in another course is allowed

Private university: A non-state-assisted college or university that relies on private funding, tuition, and fees.

Professor: Broad term for all faculty.

Public university: A state-assisted college or university

Registration: Students must enroll in classes for each semester during this time period

Resident: A student who meets state residency requirements

Resident Assistant (RA): A student leader who is responsible for supervising students living in a residence hall or dorm.

Rolling admission: When you apply to schools, find out if they have a rolling admission program. If so, apply as early as possible. A school with rolling admission will accept students as they apply and does not wait until all applications are received before they begin sending out acceptance letters.

Scholarships: A scholarship offers students financial assistance based on merit, whether academically based or based on other eligibility, and also does not require repayment.

Senior: A student who has completed 90 or more hours of college credit but has not received a bachelor's degree. In college, the years you are in school do not determine your "title." A senior might be in his sixth or seventh year of college.

Sophomore: A sophomore is a student who has completed 30 to 59 college credit hours of coursework.

Stafford Loan: A Stafford Loan is a student loan offered to eligible students enrolled in accredited American institutions. Students applying for a Stafford loan or other federal financial aid must first complete a FAFSA. No payments are expected on the loan while the student is enrolled as a full- or half-time student. This deferment continues for six months after the student leaves school either by graduating, dropping below half-time enrollment, or withdrawing.

Subsidized Loan: With these loans, the borrower is not charged interest. For this type of loan, the U.S. Department of Education pays the interest while the student is in school.

Summer session: A summer term of courses, commonly lasting six weeks

Syllabus: Written description of course content distributed by instructors to students

Teaching Assistant (TA): A junior scholar employed on a temporary contract by a college or university. TA responsibilities may include tutoring, holding office hours, grading homework or exams, leading discussion sessions, or teaching classes.

Transcript: Record of all of your courses kept by the Registrar's office

Tuition: Costs for courses, not including additional student fees

Unsubsidized Loan: These loans differ from subsidized Stafford Loans in that the student will be charged interest during the time they are in school, even though they will not have to pay on the loan until after they are out of school for six months.

Web/online registration: Registration through the internet for classes

Work-study program: A federal financial aid program that allows students to work on campus, more often than not limiting the number of hours students are allowed to work each week

Appendix

Packing List

BEDDING

- ☐ Bedbug-protecting mattress cover
- ☐ Foam topper mattress pad
- ☐ Twin XL sheet set (and an extra set)

- ☐ Duvet and duvet cover or comforter set
- ☐ Twin XL bed skirt
- ☐ Pillows
- ☐ Pillowcases
- ☐ Throw blanket

ROOM

- ☐ Bedside table
- ☐ Alarm clock
- ☐ Bedside lamp
- ☐ Floor lamp

- ☐ Area rug
- ☐ Bed risers
- ☐ Underbed storage

☐ Adhesive hooks and strips that can be removed without leaving marks

☐ Bulletin board and/or dry erase board

☐ Push pins/magnets/ whiteboard markers

☐ Wall decorations

☐ Photos

☐ Picture frames or photo clips

☐ Closet organizer

☐ Hangers

☐ Full-length mirror

☐ Trashcan

LAUNDRY

☐ Laundry hamper or bag

☐ Laundry detergent

☐ Bleach

☐ Fabric softener

☐ Stain remover

☐ Dryer sheets

☐ Iron and ironing board or handheld steamer

☐ Lint brush

☐ Sewing kit

DESK/SCHOOL SUPPLIES

☐ Backpack

☐ Binders

☐ Calculator

☐ Desk lamp

☐ Desk organizer

☐ File folder for important documents

☐ Folders

☐ Glue

☐ Notebook paper

☐ Notebooks

- [ ] Index cards
- [ ] Post-it notes
- [ ] Pencils
- [ ] Erasers
- [ ] Pens/colored pens
- [ ] Permanent marker
- [ ] Highlighters

- [ ] White-Out
- [ ] Planner
- [ ] Scissors
- [ ] Stapler
- [ ] Staples
- [ ] Staple remover
- [ ] Three-hole punch

HOUSEHOLD SUPPLIES

- [ ] Mini fridge (if your school allows it)
- [ ] Toaster (if your school allows it)
- [ ] Coffee maker (if your school allows it)
- [ ] Oven mitt
- [ ] Water filter pitcher
- [ ] Reusable water bottle
- [ ] Utensils
- [ ] Dishes (bowls, plates, cups)
- [ ] Mugs
- [ ] Travel mug

- [ ] Can opener
- [ ] Chip clips
- [ ] Food storage containers
- [ ] Plastic wrap
- [ ] Sealable plastic bags
- [ ] Tinfoil
- [ ] Dish towels
- [ ] Paper towels
- [ ] Dishwashing soap
- [ ] Hand soap
- [ ] Disinfecting wipes
- [ ] Sponges

☐ Broom and dustpan   ☐ Trash bags

☐ Mini vacuum

BATHROOM

☐ Shower mat   ☐ Loofah and/or washcloths

☐ Shower shoes

☐ Shower cap   ☐ Bath towels

☐ Shower caddy   ☐ Hand towels

Roommate Questionnaire

1. Rate how you prefer your shared living area:

   Neat & Clean   1   2   3   4   5   **Messy & Disorganized**

2. How do you typically clean: ☐ Clean right away   ☐ Clean before I go to bed/within 24 hours   ☐ I wait a few days

3. Do you consider yourself: **Shy**   1   2   3   4   5   **Outgoing**

4. I will probably be at my apartment: ☐ A majority of the time ☐ I may be gone most weekends   ☐ I will hardly be home

5. Describe your alcohol use: ☐ Never   ☐ A few times a month ☐ 1-2 times week   ☐ 3-5 days week   ☐ 6-7 days week

6. Do you mind if your roommates drink? ☐ Prefer no alcohol   ☐ 1-3 times week OK   ☐ Weekends OK   ☐ Any time OK

7. Do you smoke?   ☐ Yes   ☐ No

8. Do you mind if your roommates are smokers?   ☐ Yes   ☐ No

9. How often do you plan on having guests in the apartment?

   _____

10. How often may your roommates have guests in the apartment?

   _____

11. How much of your free time do you spend listening to music?

   ☐ Most of the time   ☐ Occasionally   ☐ Rarely

12. What are your musical preferences? Check all that apply:

   ☐ Country ☐ Rock, ☐ Rap/Hip Hop ☐ Jazz ☐ Alternative ☐ R&B ☐ Classical ☐ Talk ☐ Other _____

13. How much time do you spend watching television each day? ☐ Rarely ☐ 1-3 hours   ☐ 3-5 hours   ☐ 5-8 hours

14. Your favorite television show? _____

15. Do you play a musical instrument for a hobby? _____

16. My favorite sport or team is _____

17. Do you have any special allergies or dietary restrictions?

_____

18. If there is a problem I prefer it's communicated to me: ☐ In a note
☐ Talk to me directly   ☐ Text me   ☐ Other _____

19. When do typically you start your day? Check the time that applies:

☐ 7 am or earlier   ☐ 8-9 am   ☐ 10-11 am   ☐ Noon or later

20. When do you typically go to bed? Check the time that applies:

☐ 9 pm   ☐ 10pm   ☐ 11pm   ☐ Midnight   ☐ 1 am or later

21. Please check all that describe your study habits: ☐ Perfectionist
☐ I like to do what I need to get by   ☐ Organized   ☐ Disorganized
☐ Last-minute, stay up all night   ☐ Plan ahead   ☐ Like to study at
night   ☐ Like to study during the day   ☐ Like to study with music
☐ Like to study in complete silence   ☐ Like to study in groups
☐ Prefer to study alone   ☐ Other: _____

22. What are some of your extracurricular interests? _____

_____

23. Do you plan on joining a fraternity or a sorority? _____

24. What are you looking for in a roommate? _____

_____

25. Any additional comments, questions, or concerns _____

_____

Bibliography

ACHANCHA, "Undergraduate Student Reference Group." *American College Health Association National College Health Assessment,* American College Health Association, 2016, http://www.acha-ncha.org/docs/NCHA-II_FALL_2016_UNDERGRADUATE_REFERENCE_GROUP_EXECUTIVE_SUMMARY.pdf.

Anonymous. "Alcohol and the Law: Minor in Possession (MIP) and Fake ID." *UC Berkeley: Division of Student Affairs*, UC Regents, 13 Nov. 2015, sa.berkeley.edu/legal/tipsheet/alcohol

Big Future. "Financial Aid: FAQs." *Big Future,* The College Board, n.d., https://bigfuture.collegeboard.org/pay-for-college/financial-aid-101/financial-aid-faqs.

"Campus Sexual Violence: Statistics." *RAINN*, Rape, Abuse & Incest National Network, 2016, www.rainn.org/statistics/campus-sexual-violence.

Chuck, Elizabeth. "Match Made on Facebook: More College Freshmen Choose Their Own Roommates." *NBC News,* NBC News, 26 June, 2015, https://www.nbcnews.com/feature/freshman-year/match-made-facebook-more-college-students-choosing-their-roommates-n381036.

Dobbs, Kevin. "Why college student and employers pursue internships as a path to future employment." *Deseret News,* Deseret News, 11 May 2016, https://www.deseretnews.com/article/865653969/Why-college-students-and-employers-pursue-internships-as-a-path-to-future-employment.html.

Ellis, Blake. "Average Student Loan Debt Nears $27,000." *CNNMoney,* Cable News Network, 18 Oct. 2012, money.cnn.com/2012/10/18/pf/college/student-loan-debt/index.html.

"Facts About Alcohol Overdose (or Alcohol Poisoning)." *College Drinking: Changing the Culture,* National Institute on Alcohol Abuse and Alcoholism, www.collegedrinkingprevention.gov/ParentsandStudents/Students/FactSheets/factsAboutAlcoholPoisoning.aspx.

Fay, Max. "Paying Back Student Loans." *Debt.org,* America's Debt Help Organization, 11 Jul. 2017, https://www.debt.org/students/how-to-pay-back-loans/.

Geary , Leslie Haggan. "Scholarships Are out There. You Just Need to Look." *CNNMoney,* Cable News Network, 24 July 2002, money.cnn.com/2002/06/11/pf/college/q_scholarship/.

Glass, Nicole. "Examining the benefits of Greek Life." *USA Today College,* USA Today, 8 May, 2012, http://college.usatoday.com/2012/05/08/examining-the-benefits-of-greek-life/.

"Loans." *Federal Student Aid,* U.S. Department of Education, 21 Feb. 2017, studentaid.ed.gov/sa/types/loans.

"Major Decisions: Facts & Figures about Students Changing Majors." *University Exploration,* University of Ohio State, exploration.osu.edu/

"Major Exploration." *Career Services,* University of La Verne, sites.laverne.edu/careers/what-can-i-do-with-my-major/

Makridis, Christos. "Does it pay to get a double major?" *Quartz*, Quartz, 30 March. 2017, https://qz.com/945083/new-research-suggests-it-really-does-pay-to-get-a-double-major-in-college/.

"Meningococcal Disease: Information for Teens and College Students." *Healthy Children*, American Academy of Pediatrics , 2016, www.healthychildren.org/English/ages-stages/teen/Pages/Meningococcal-Disease-Information-for-Teens-and-College-Students-.aspx.

NAFSA, "Trends in U.S. Study Abroad." *National Association of Foreign Student Advisors*, NAFSA: Association of International Educators, n.d., http://www.nafsa.org/Policy_and_Advocacy/Policy_Resources/Policy_Trends_and_Data/Trends_in_U_S__Study_Abroad/.

NIAAA. "College Drinking." *National Institute on Alcohol Abuse and Alcoholism*, National Institutes of Health, n.d., https://pubs.niaaa.nih.gov/publications/collegefactsheet/Collegefactsheet.pdf.

Rapacon, Stacy. "More college students are working while studying." *CNBC*, NBCUniversal News Group, 29 Oct. 2015, https://www.cnbc.com/2015/10/29/more-college-students-are-working-while-studying.html.

"Repay Loans." *Federal Student Aid*, U.S. Department of Education, 21 Feb. 2017, https://studentaid.ed.gov/sa/repay-loans.

Schweers, Jeffrey. "Hand, foot and mouth disease hits FSU." *Tallahassee Democrat*, USA Today Network, 14 Sept. 2016, http://www.tallahassee.com/story/news/2016/09/14/university-officials-respond-to-hand-foot-and-mouth-disease/90350756/.

Simon, Cecilia Capuzzi. "Major Decisions." *The New York Times*, The New York Times, 3 Nov. 2012, www.nytimes.com/2012/11/04/education/edlife/choosing-one-college-major-out-of-hundreds.html.

Straumsheim, Carl. "Study finds students benefit from waiting to declare a major." *Insider Higher Ed,* Insider Higher Ed, 24 Aug. 2016, https://www.insidehighered.com/news/2016/08/24/study-finds-students-benefit-waiting-declare-major.

Strayer, Nick. "The Great Out-of-State Migration: Where Students Go." *The New York Times*, The New York Times, 26 Aug. 2016, https://www.nytimes.com/interactive/2016/08/26/us/college-student-migration.html.

Student Activities and Involvement. "Student Organizations." *Department of Student Activities and Involvement,* Division of Student Affairs University of Florida, 2017, https://www.studentinvolvement.ufl.edu/Student-Organizations.

Texas A&M University. "Studying: Is it bad for your health to pull an all-nighter?." *ScienceDaily*. ScienceDaily, 19 Sept. 2016, www.sciencedaily.com/releases/2016/09/160919162837.htm.

"Understanding How Credit Card Interest Works." *Discover*, Discover Bank, 21 July 2017, www.discover.com/credit-cards/resources/how-does-my-credit-card-interest-work.

"What is Consent?" RAINN, Rape, Abuse & Incest National Network, 2016, www.rainn.org/statistics/campus-sexual-violence.https://www.rainn.org/articles/what-is-consent.

"Why Study Abroad?" *USA Study Abroad*, U.S. Department of State, 5 June 2017, studyabroad.state.gov/experience-studying-abroad/why-study-abroad.

Wilson, Tim. "How to Use Daily Planners Effectively." *Time Management Success*, Tim Wilson, 2017, http://www.time-management-success.com/daily-planners.html.

Wong, Kristin. "Freshman Homesickness: What Can You Do To Combat This Freshmen Malady." *NBC News*, National Broadcasting Company, 23 Oct 2015, https://www.nbcnews.com/feature/freshman-year/freshman-homesickness-what-you-can-do-combat-common-malady-n450266.

"Work-Study Jobs." *Federal Student Aid*, U.S. Department of Education, 23 Aug. 2017, studentaid.ed.gov/sa/types/work-study#what-kinds-of-jobs.

Index

About the Author

Danielle is a recent college graduate from the University of Florida, which is why she was able to provide you all with such quality advice. She graduated with a degree in advertising and a minor in English and currently works as a project manager and editor. When not writing books, she can usually be found reading them.

She currently resides in Gainesville, FL—graduating only means they kick you out of the college, not the college town.